# Personal Transformation through Reiki

Tom Radzienda
Reiki Thailand

# Personal Transformation through Reiki
Copyright © 2018 by Tom Radzienda
All rights reserved

### Published in Thai language as:
เรกิ พลังธรรมชาติ

Copyright © 2017 by Tom Radzienda

This book is a **Sovereign Word** Publication

ISBN 978-616-321-420-1

CIP 55-29856

### Legal Rights and Responsibilities

Reiki is for the benefit of all. This book is for the benefit of all. Please respect the essence of Reiki and the rights of the author by not reproducing this book without permission. Brief passages may be quoted, translated or reproduced for educational or non-profit purposes with written permission from the author. Otherwise, no part of this book can be reproduced or transmitted in any form or by any means.

### Disclaimer

The ideas and suggestions in "Personal Transformation through Reiki" are intended for educational purposes. The information provided in this book is for healing purposes and does not constitute medical advice. This book is not intended to replace medical advice, or to diagnose, prescribe or treat any disease, condition or injury.

# Table of Contents

**Preface and Acknowledgements**   vii

**Foreword**   ix

**Chapter One: Welcome to Reiki**   1

    How does Reiki Work?
    Do I have to believe in Reiki for it to Work?
    Is there Research to prove the effects of Reiki?
    Is Reiki just a Placebo?
    Reiki History
    The Reiki Attunement
    Is Reiki a Religion?
    What is the source of Reiki?
    Quantum Physics and Reiki
    Conclusion

**Chapter Two: Becoming a Reiki Channel**   21

    Reiki Principles
    Benefits of Reiki
    Is Reiki Safe?
    Meditation for Reiki
    Conclusion

**Chapter Three: Training and Healing with Reiki 1**   37

    Self Healing
    When to give Reiki
    Giving Reiki
    Blessings
    Sensing Energy

Sweeping and Scanning
Healing Positions
Duration of Healing
Balancing the Chakras
Closing the Aura
Grounding
Reflecting on a Healing Session
After completing your Reiki Training Course
Reiki for Animals
Additional Healing Techniques
Conclusion

## Chapter Four: Knowledge and Experience of Chakras    57

Root Chakra
Navel (Sacral) Chakra
Solar Plexus Chakra
Heart Chakra
Throat Chakra
Brow Chakra
Crown Chakra
Acupressure
Guided Chakra Meditation
Positive Affirmation Meditation
Connecting the Chakras
Chakra Spread
Conclusion

## Chapter Five: Reiki 2 Symbols and Procedures    87

Attunement to Reiki 2
Reiki Symbols
Drawing and Visualising Symbols
Cho Ku Rei: The Power Symbol
Sei He Ki: The Emotional Symbol
Hon Sha Ze Sho Nen: The Distance Symbol
Hands-on Healing with Reiki 2
The Healing Process

Therapeutic Communication
Sending Reiki to the Origin of Issues
Closing the Healing Process
After Healing is Complete

## Chapter Six: Advanced Reiki 2 — 105

Distance Healing
Distance Healing to your Younger Self
Healing and Manifesting through Written Request
Self Knowledge
Personal Insight through Reiki
Using a Pendulum with Reiki
Calibrating your Pendulum
Reading with your Pendulum
Reading the Energy of Chakras with a Pendulum
Using Crystals with Reiki
Conclusion

## Chapter Seven:
## A Holistic approach to Personal Development — 123

Pranayama
Activating Breath
Calming Breath
Alternate Nostril Breathing
Breath of Fire
Inter-Disciplinary Chakra Energising Routine
Becoming the Breath
Taiji
Microcosmic Orbit
Summary
Dimensions of Health

## Chapter Eight: Natural Healing, Healing Nature — 141

Naturopathy and Reiki
Naturopathy and Fasting
Naturopathy and Water

Naturopathy and Air
Naturopathy and Sunlight
Naturopathy and Earth
Naturopathy and Food
Veganism and Reiki
Hormones and Pesticides in your Diet
The Production of Meat
Animal Slaughter
Digestion and your Health
Veganism and Personal Health
The Vegan Transition
Veganism and Spiritual Practice
Veganism and Planetary Healing
Conclusion

## Chapter Nine: Planetary Transformation     165

Beyond Self
Transforming yourself through Relationships
Transformation of Social Attitudes
Written Meditation
Healing Community
Planetary Health Care
Planetary Responsibilities
Universal Meditation
Blessings

## Afterword     179

## Annotated Bibliography     181

## About the Author     187

# Preface and Acknowledgements

My personal path for the last several years has involved exploring where poetry meets healing. I've been practising Reiki for nearly ten years and writing poetry for more than thirty years. I increasingly recognise that the intuition, symbols and images in poetry parallel the work that I conduct with Reiki. In both pursuits, I am seeking wisdom and wholeness. In poetry, this involves insight and epiphany. In Reiki, it's called intuition and healing.

When writing poetry, I'm searching for essence within myself and in our world. I seek the primordial source of wisdom, penetrating to the roots of existence. This search has taken me all over Asia, Africa, Europe and the Americas, and more importantly, into the quarry of my own being. The search involves Reiki, Vipassana meditation, fasting and spiritual healing.

Poetry means a lifetime of self-discovery. I write feverishly until I discover the answers for which I yearn. Once written, I recognise my personal vision and beyond; I tune in to universal awareness by abandoning a personal perspective and merging into a sense of infinity. Teaching and healing with Reiki represent a very similar path: Reiki takes me beyond self into a universe of energy that transcends human comprehension.

Early in my Reiki training, I focused on healing the aches and pains of life that many of us face, including depression, dependence on alcohol, anger, back problems and deeply rooted stress. Reiki, meditation, Yoga, Taiji and fasting helped me process my personal challenges and gain further insight into the roots of my human foibles. Experiential suffering and healing have served as a personal training programme that has made me healthy and strong enough to heal others addressing their own personal challenges.

Poetry, like Reiki, began for me as a very personal quest and has since expanded into a community service. For further reading, you may be interested in my most recent collection of poetry, "Luxuries of Grace" and my latest spiritual book, "Essence." I'm very pleased to share my Reiki experiences with you in the present book. I hope I can support you in your personal transformation.

Many thanks to all the people who have contributed so much to this book. Many friends have provided insightful advice including Ralph Achenbach, Eric Dubay, Kit Johnson and Nicole Lasas. Even on points where we disagree, their input has been priceless in keeping me in line. Also thanks to Kowittaya Meeponsom for his friendship and excellent photography.

Thanks to our translation and editing team without whom the Thai version of this book would never have come into existence: Pairin Jotisakulratana, Dadchaneevan Uhlig, Dao Wipasirin, Zuwannie Jariyayothin, Sutassi Smuthkochorn, Pracha Hutanuwatr and Chofa Jettanaveerabut. Special thanks to Pisamai U-Pratya who has helped at every stage of the writing, translating and producing of this book.

Writing this book in both Thai and English languages has been a tremendous growing experience. It has become so clear that this is "our" book much more than being "my" book. This insight has made all the difference in the manuscript, in practice and in my own being.

I thank all my teachers, students, clients and friends who have richly contributed to my Reiki experience. Thanks to Carol Knox of the Arura Reiki Centre in South Africa for her support and guidance. I thank all of my other teachers, known and unknown, who have passed Reiki along to me over the last hundred years. My Reiki lineage can be traced from Dr. Mikao Usui to Dr. Chujiro Hayashi to Hawayo Takata to Iris Ishikuro to Arthur Robertson to Glenda Rye to Karen Miller to Alexis Summerfield to Pierre Wittmann to my personal teacher Danielle Wiedmann who continues to support me with her friendship and enthusiasm. I pass this gift to all my students, all my readers and to all we heal…

Tom Radzienda<br>
Bangkok, Thailand

# Foreword

Tom and I have been travelling companions on a spiritual journey for many years. We meditate together, lead workshops together and converse every chance we get. He is insightful concerning contemporary Western society, recognising that it is much healthier and wiser to live outside the mainstream and forego extensive opportunities to "succeed" by Western social values.

I am pleased that he has narrated his Reiki story in such an interesting and enjoyable format. He has amalgamated diverse wisdom from China and India into his vision of personal development and healing. His holistic approach to Reiki draws on Taoism, Taiji, Buddhism, Yoga, Naturopathy and Pranayama. He effectively synthesises these disciplines into his practise and teaching of Reiki natural healing for the benefit of his students and readers. He has included vital references in the writing of this book, yet the essence reveals his characteristic insight and personal experience. What we gain from the book is not simply theory, but authentic experiences recounted in a clear, engaging style.

Tom has accomplished the mission of his book because he has earnestly healed himself to attain optimum personal health and balance in his life. He represents a generation of people who are honest about life and arduously seeking its deeper meaning. He has lived, learned and taught here in Thailand for two decades along with his wife who shares his conviction and commitment to personal and global well-being.

Readers may or may not agree with the social and scientific concepts presented in these pages, but will certainly find the ideas and perspectives to be thought provoking. The point is to practise the techniques described in this book and determine for yourself how well they work from you. You will gain a wider perspective and deeper insight into yourself, society and the world.

Tom has compiled diverse aspects of knowledge concerning health and spiritual care that he has effectively applied in his own development. He blends these into a challenging new vision for promoting a higher quality of life centring on Reiki. Even if Reiki is not your chosen field, you will still find the book constructive in considering new perspectives that are far-reaching, beautiful and friendly. You may be interested in Pranayama or chakras as they relate to psychology and personal development. Some may be interested in the use of pendulums or crystals and discover new ideas concerning healthcare, nutrition and pharmaceuticals. Others may be interested in Reiki for body, soul and spirituality.

E. F. Schumacher, in his significant work "The Guide for the Perplexed" warned that mechanistic science is limited to convergent knowledge which is materialistic and measurable. It may be great for developing space craft and sophisticated computer systems, but hardly nurtures our humanity. Wisdom concerning humankind such as health, morality, equality, justice, love, happiness and grief represent divergent knowledge. These dimensions of our lives simply can't be quantified or objectified in the manner of material science. To be candid, divergent knowledge is far more important to humanity. Due to the current education system, most of the world fails to appreciate the significance of divergent knowledge, so busy are we manipulating the world through the paradigms of mechanical science.

"Personal Transformation through Reiki" emphasises divergent knowledge without being blind to the contributions of the mechanistic worldview. Those who seek divergent knowledge require deep, dedicated training of the mind to attain advanced levels of understanding. Therefore, I am thankful that Tom has written this book. The reading public will gain greater insight into alternative approaches to well-being that are radically different from reductionist, mechanistic approaches to health care.

It is commendable that Tom recognises the contribution of scientific health treatment without falling into the traps of mechanistic allopathic health practices. He proposes that health care must be considered wisely from multiple perspectives dealing with numerous dimensions.

This book has been delightfully welcomed in the Thai reading community, coming just at the right time when Thai consciousness is yearning to awaken. I trust this book will be equally welcomed in the English speaking world.

> Pracha Hutanuwatra
> Bangkok, Thailand

Pracha Hutanuwatra is the author of "The Asian Future: Dialogues for Change" and four books in Thai, including "Spirituality and the Search of the New Generation."

# Chapter One

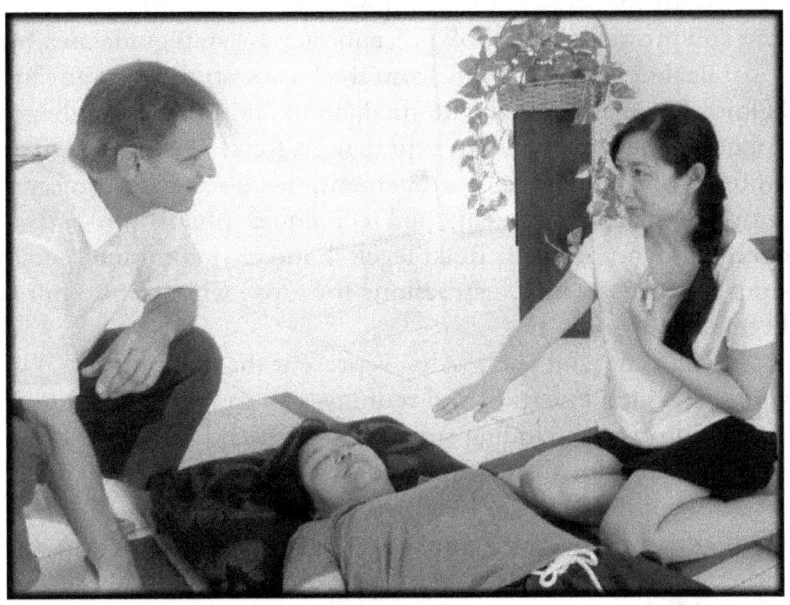

# Welcome to Reiki

"What is Reiki? What do you mean by universal energy? Can it be measured? Can you prove it?" You could read a hundred books on Reiki and still not know, still not understand and still not believe in it. On the other hand, after just a few minutes of receiving Reiki healing, you'll know that Reiki is warm, comforting and healing. The proof of Reiki is when you experience the energy flowing through your body and mind. The measure of Reiki is how widely you are willing to open your mind and how brave you are to make the changes that Reiki facilitates. But maybe you don't believe me...

"Personal Transformation through Reiki" presents a holistic perspective of the world of Reiki: how it works and how to use it for healing and growth. This book presents step by step guidelines for personal healing/development from the basics up through advanced Reiki knowledge integrated with meditation and other life enhancing disciplines. While you need an experienced Reiki Master to activate your power of Reiki through attunement, this book makes every attempt to explain the fundamental techniques, philosophy and practices that you need for Reiki levels 1 and 2. It combines personal experiences with detailed instructions for those who wish to pursue Reiki training.

Reiki is natural energy that is present throughout the universe. Through initiation and training, you can focus this energy for many purposes, including spiritual growth and healing. Reiki balances the emotional and intellectual aspects of your being. It harmonises spiritual energies with your physical self. Reiki brings all elements of your being into tune. Further, it brings your entire being into tune with the universe. It nurtures your understanding of oneness with the universe and helps you holistically perceive life in all its dimensions and manifestations. Reiki is used for healing yourself; healing others; and connecting to meta-physical spiritual energies through powerful initiation ceremonies.

Reiki helps you become aware of spiritual reality by directly experiencing the warmth and vibration of high energy. It opens your mental, spiritual and emotional channels to deepen spiritual perception. Reiki is supportive of spiritual growth by bringing deeper insight during meditation. It is used for healing spiritual issues, emotional blocks and physical illnesses. No, you don't have to "believe" in Reiki, but please, unplug any "disbelief" because this severely restricts comprehension. I would like to challenge your perception of the world so that you can liberate yourself from any limiting beliefs. I encourage you to embrace a holistic perspective towards your personal and planetary health. I hope to inspire profound insights into the nature of reality and self through the practice of Reiki. Please open your heart and mind for the experience of a lifetime in touch with Reiki.

# How does Reiki Work?

"So how does Reiki work?" Every student asks me this question and I invariably answer in a different way every time, even though the basic concept remains the same. Reiki works in the same way that everything works; that is, consistent with the laws of nature. No, I don't mean the laws of science that we learned at school, but the laws of nature that transcend classical scientific theories.

The truth is that orthodox conceptions of human nature and human beings are terribly reductionist and narrow. Through material empiricism, our species has somehow been reduced to atomistic electro-mechanical machines consisting of nothing more than elements and chemicals simmering inside of our bodies. Material empiricism amounts to material fundamentalism. When we expand our awareness and deepen our consciousness, the concept and experience of Reiki become quite evident. Reiki is supremely simple to experience, but extremely difficult to explain.

Sure, the procedures, techniques and history of Reiki are straight forward and easy to understand, but the question of how Reiki works can be mysterious and beyond the comprehension of rational, scientific thought. A powerful observation by physicist Sir James Jeans in 1930 explains that the universe looks more like a "great thought than like a great machine." In the last 80 years, physicists have proven this to be the case with one experiment after another. From this world view, universal interconnectedness and the power of consciousness become exponentially more important: Consciousness influences matter. Thoughts of healing a person bring forth healing. Thought influences thought, and we are all thought, so we all influence everything! Does this sound like hocus-pocus? Be sure to review your understanding of quantum physics very carefully before arriving at such a conclusion.

Reiki heals at the spiritual, emotional, intellectual and physical levels of being by transforming blocked or negative patterns into positive, flowing energy. Remember, everything is energy: Mass is energy. Fire is energy. Atoms and particles are energy. Healthy and unhealthy thoughts are energy. Love and hate are energy. The physical human body is an energy vibrating at a low frequency. The conscious and spiritual aspects of humans vibrate at higher frequencies. The difference between these types of phenomena depends on the frequency of vibrations. To claim that some realms do not exist because we cannot see them is sort of like claiming that a high frequency sound beyond 20,000 Hertz does not exist because we cannot hear it. Bear in mind, human intellect is hardly the ultimate measure of the universe. More likely, human intellect may be one of our greatest barriers to apprehending the universe.

Thought influences matter just as mind influences body. High frequency mental and spiritual energy may not be directly perceptible to our physical sense organs, but the effects of mental activity manifest in numerous physical conditions. Many ailments such as headaches and ulcers are a physical response to mental energies. Similarly, smiles and laughter are physical responses to positive emotional energy. When you understand yourself in this way, it makes sense that Reiki can stimulate physical improvements to your health.

Reiki is a compassionate energy similar to the positive energy generated by meditation, love or prayer. All of these vibrate on higher frequencies, bringing forth changes in physical being. Studies have shown that communities around meditation centres experience lower levels of crime. So, the influence of positive energy extends from self, to community to humanity as a whole.

It's no surprise that when a student comes for a Reiki healing after years of stomach problems, back pain or headaches, one Reiki treatment can reveal that they have been unconsciously holding negative energy such as fear, anger or guilt. Negativity gets locked up in the digestive organs, trapped in the muscles or embedded in the brain, blocking the natural flow of energy. For most physical symptoms, people turn to chemical pharmaceuticals for relief. When the cause of a headache or an ulcer is mental or emotional, all the drugs in the world will fail to heal the root cause. Drugs may provide temporary relief by masking or suppressing symptoms, but they rarely get to the origins of disease.

Why has modern society reduced its concept of the human body to mere chemical equations? Why don't we perceive ourselves in our totality and address our health in terms of our total being? This is what Reiki and other holistic healing modes aim to accomplish. The amazing thing is that classical science perceives the world in terms of cause and effect because of the scientific method that it applies, not because of the nature of reality! Similarly, the things we observe in a healing situation, be it allopathic or energetic, depend on our method of observation. When a chemist sets up an experiment, chemical reactions are observed. Conversely, when a Reiki healer arranges a healing, energetic responses are observed. So, which one is real? Maybe nothing is real until you try it and experience it yourself. This conception is consistent with post-modern notions of multiple truths and scientific notions of quantum physics.

Reiki healers open their minds and hearts to channel healing energy. By placing hands on another student, Reiki is channelled through consciousness to remove or transform unhealthy or blocked energies that cause illness. Reiki increases harmony with the universe, generating sensations of lightness, brightness and compassion. As Gena said when she received her first healing, "I feel like I'm spirit." I gently reminded her that she was, indeed, spirit. Reiki confirmed for her through a very concrete, sensory experience of lightness and calmness that humans are first and foremost spiritual beings.

### Do I have to believe in Reiki for it to Work?

"I don't believe it!" Many people don't believe it! Ironically, "disbelief" in itself can be a very firm belief. The odd thing is that most of us "believe" in electro-magnetic force and gravity, without having any deep understanding how these forces work. Who knows if those are just theories or if they really exist? All we know for sure is that the computer works when turned on and cups of coffee never go floating around your kitchen. When was the last time you met someone who refused to plug in a computer because they didn't believe in the second law of thermodynamics? Understanding Reiki has very little to do with belief. It just works, that's it, in the same way that gravity holds down my cup of coffee even though I disagree with Newton.

Orthodox physics can honestly claim that they are unable to measure Reiki, but this is definitely not the same as saying that Reiki does not exist. If any scientist makes the latter claim, it demonstrates nothing more than a dogmatic game of peek-a-boo that denies all things that cannot be measured. After all, who authorised orthodox scientists to determine the nature and boundaries of our existence?

"Reiki still seems so out of reach. Is it that complex and difficult?" No, not really. If you're having a conversation with somebody who knows Reiki, you are already within arm's reach of experience. The only remaining question is whether or not you reach out to receive it. Reiki is intended to be experienced and sensed, from which understanding follows. If you spend years reading and researching Reiki, you may never arrive at any true appreciation of it and how it can benefit you; you may never appreciate in a visceral sense that everything is energy.

Explaining Reiki is sort of like trying to explain God. You can theorise about God all day long and never come close to personal knowledge until you sit silently in meditation or prayer and experience God viscerally through your whole being, rather than academically or intellectually. Simply put, God is neither an academic subject nor an intellectual pursuit, although people through the ages have been known to pursue those paths.

Similarly, Reiki needs to be approached intuitively rather than rationally. Indeed, it may be necessary to suspend your rational beliefs long enough to perceive the severe restrictions of rationality. One friend wrote me an e-mail saying, "Hi Tom, nice to hear from u & thanks for info on Reiki course... although would like to be more convinced of its efficacy... any chance of a demonstration?" I wrote back to him:

> I would be happy to do a session of Reiki with you. The first thing to ask is how open you are to this process. Ask yourself, and estimate, hey, how much am I willing to believe or accept this thing? Sure, belief is a factor, but not for the reasons claimed by "realists" who define any unexplainable results as a placebo effect.
>
> More importantly, a refusal to believe creates a situation where a person is unable to perceive, thus confirming their doubts, which many people mistakenly consider to be proof that something doesn't exist. When we open, we lower our barriers, and allow spirit to present itself to us.
>
> So, if a guy believes only 20% in something, then he will consequently only be able to receive about 20% of the energy, and would then logically deduce that the energy or spirit is only about 20% effective. The reasons for refusing to believe or for blocking energy are many. If for example, a person was estranged from their country, and Reiki was bringing up this issue through the intuition of the healer, then the receiver would subconsciously or psychically block that energy flow in order to block that intuitive information. This would effectively prevent the issue from arising

because it might be too threatening to the patient at that time, e.g. they are not yet ready to heal those deep issues.

I wrote that email more than three years ago and my friend has somewhat predictably still not taken me up on my offer to give him Reiki. I suspect that maybe the example I suggested in my mail is too close to the heart and he is not truly ready to experience Reiki; not because he doesn't believe, but because subconsciously, he fears that it may be real and he fears that it will truly raise painful issues that he has hidden from himself in his own heart.

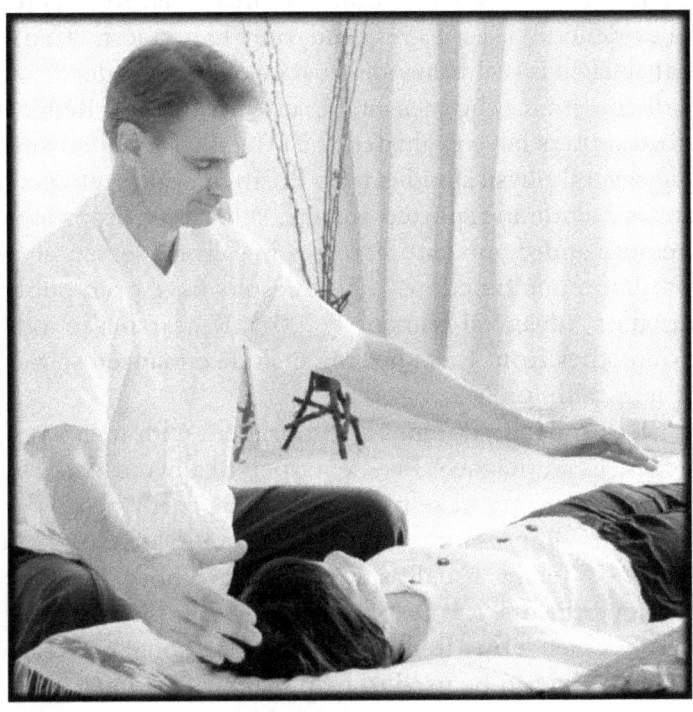

## Is there Research to prove the Effects of Reiki?

"Can you prove that Reiki works?" What kind of proof would you prefer? Volumes of research, data and personal anecdotes have been compiled from all over the world for more than fifty years on topics such as ESP, spontaneous healing and psychic communication. Yet, somehow, all of these phenomena are still considered unscientific and unproven. In fact, such meta-physical events are in perfect tune with the laws of quantum physics. Research concerning energy and consciousness is often more thorough, arduous and demanding than research by pharmaceutical corporations that market highly toxic drugs that can lead to death.

When somebody asks, "Can you prove that Reiki is real using empirical evidence?" I like to respond, only half in jest, "Can you prove that science is real using spiritual evidence?" Indeed, academic research demonstrates the measurable effectiveness of Reiki.

Researchers have evaluated the effects of Reiki on stress by measuring several physical indicators. Positive healing effects include significant reduction in reported anxiety, significant drops in systolic blood pressure and significant increases in salivary secretions relating to increased immune functions. These results have been published in the "Journal of Advanced Nursing" (2001). Research also indicates positive outcomes from Reiki healing include enhanced self-esteem and increased faith in God.

These academic findings are consistent with my own experience of Reiki practice. I've never personally measured a patient's blood pressure or salivary secretions, partly because I don't know how. More importantly, I don't measure those factors because the influence of Reiki is usually quite evident to both healer and recipient. Nevertheless, it is helpful to know that the academic community is considering Reiki seriously. Additional research explains how Reiki can be used to help diabetes patients.

Diabetes is when the body is unable to metabolise food products sufficiently. According to Registered Nurse Kathie Lipinski, "Reiki can be thought of as balancing and healing all aspects of one's being." She encourages all her clients with diabetes to learn Reiki to stay healthy and cope with the stresses of everyday life. She explains that stress throws the blood sugar out of balance and can cause higher than normal blood sugar. Reiki minimises the effects of stress. She adds that the hands can be placed over the solar plexus (see chapter 4) where the pancreas is located to nourish it and relieve any stress gathered there. A word of caution; a person with diabetes who receives Reiki regularly needs to be aware of its effect on blood sugar levels. Due to the relaxation induced by Reiki, it may be necessary to adjust the dosage of insulin or diabetes medicine. The same is true with patients taking medicine for high blood pressure. In both cases, patients are advised to consult with their physicians to determine if any adjustments are needed in their dosage. This research presents a valuable example of allopathic and alternative healing approaches being used together wisely and cautiously by a health professional. Use of one healing approach does not negate the option of using another as evidenced by the use of Reiki in hospitals.

Reiki is gaining recognition in hospitals around the world. Seventy hospitals in the UK, US, Egypt, Argentina, Belgium and Canada provide health care with Reiki. In a study published in 2007 in "Issues in Mental Health Nursing," registered nurses enrolled to study Reiki and kept journals of their experiences. The main things observed at the physical level included sensations of warmth, pulsations and calmness. In occupational terms, the nurses reported enhanced problem solving ability and increased ability to focus on patient needs. The nurses consistently reported feeling more positive about their work after participating in Reiki self healing classes. It's encouraging to know that the nursing profession is recognising and using Reiki in its health care practices.

It's a blessing that more professions are opening the discourse to the benefits of Reiki. Meanwhile, I suggest that you don't wait for the academic or medical professions to declare whether Reiki is effective or not. The real proof is when you open yourself to the experience and feel for yourself what scientists frequently are unable to measure using all the technology in the world. The only technology you really need to experience Reiki is your own body and mind.

## Is Reiki just a Placebo?

It's very peculiar that when scientists research the effects of Reiki, they tend to conclude that the effects are no more than what would be expected from a placebo. We've been led to believe that there is something wrong with the placebo effect, something suspicious that we should not trust. In "Spontaneous Healing," Dr. Andrew Weil describes how most doctors dislike placebo effects because they cause complications in their experiments. These doctors prefer "real treatments that work through identifiable biochemical mechanisms." "Placebo effects" are invoked whenever direct causation cannot be measured scientifically. Dr. Weil enthusiastically embraces placebo effects, regarding them as pure examples of healing elicited through the power of the mind. Rather than seeing this as a nuisance, Dr. Weil sees placebo effects as a "therapeutic ally" to heal disease. Have we forgotten that people heal naturally without dangerous chemicals and without actually understanding the vehicle of causation? Remember, the human body has remarkable built-in healing mechanisms.

On the other hand, consider the use of a best selling pharmaceutical drug used to treat migraines: Imitrex. This drug is never criticised as merely being a placebo. Instead, we receive a meagre disclaimer that Imitrex may cause "cardiovascular side effects including serious, sometimes **fatal** cardiac events such as ventricular fibrillation [uncoordinated contractions of the heart muscles], transient myocardial ischemia [reduced blood supply to the heart], and coronary artery vasospasm [constriction of the coronary artery]… Serious and/or life threatening arrhythmias including atrial fibrillation [abnormal heart rhythm], ventricular tachycardia [fast heart rhythm], myocardial infarction [heart attack]… thrombophlebitis [vein inflammation], angiodema [swelling similar to hives], cerebrovascular accident [stroke], pulmonary embolism [sudden blockage in a lung artery], shock, subarachnoid haemorrhage [bleeding on the brain associated with an aneurism], hypertension, bradycardia [slow heart rate], and precordial [in front of the heart] distress have also been reported."

The paltry response to this list of potential side effects is that "all drugs have side effects." And therefore, it's okay to take them??? The example of Imitrex is by no means an exception. A little cursory research on practically every pharmaceutical drug will yield equally scary results. Scientific, medical "logic" might be summarised as follows: Taking pharmaceuticals drugs that have known side effects including death is more scientific, and is therefore preferable, to seeking alternative healing modalities such as Reiki because the latter may be nothing more than a placebo effect. Am I exaggerating these dangers? I suggest you research this matter for yourself and find out what all those big words in fine print on your medicine labels really mean.

Is there any curiosity about why so many people express relief from headaches and migraines after receiving Reiki? Many people subjectively report relief, but does this qualify as science? Me, I would much prefer "subjective" relief from my headache using Reiki than take the pharmaceutical risk of "objective" life threatening atrial fibrillation. One thing that science has truly proven is that a lot of people suffer strokes, angina or die from taking migraine medicine. Is this preferable to "messing around" with natural approaches?

Now, if you find yourself involved in a serious car accident, please don't drive to the nearest Reiki clinic! Please, in the case of an accident, broken bones, burns and other acute cases, the allopathic profession has done miracles to save hundreds of thousands of lives. At the same time, be aware that tens of thousands of deaths are caused by misuse of prescription drugs. Even more shocking is that hundreds of thousands of people die in the United States each year alone due to "proper" use of physician prescribed drugs. All of these deaths indicate tremendous "faith" in pharmaceuticals, yet those pills are still marketed as "science."

"Faith in pharmaceuticals is firmly embedded in modern culture at the ideological level." Ironically, this happens in the very societies that pride themselves on being rational, objective and empirical. This blind faith is physically risky and psychologically disempowering at the same time. "Death by Prescription" by Dr. Ray Strand thoroughly explains the toxic truth of the dangers of pharmaceuticals. Chemicals are accepted as medicine, by definition. Patients are perceived more as passive objects of a chemical experiment than as active participants, mentally and physically, in their own well being. Blind faith in modern chemical warfare on our bodies is standard operating procedure in most countries.

In all events, you need to have the wisdom, knowledge and insight to make the most suitable decisions concerning health care for you, your family and your community. You need to be aware of the strengths, weaknesses, side effects and applicability of any health care measures that you consider. If you have never considered the financial interests of Wall Street in perpetuating faith in pharmaceuticals, read "Selling Sickness" by Ray Moynihan and Alan Cassels. They provide a thought provoking analysis of diseases that are invented or manufactured for mass consumption and therefore, for mass medication.

It's your body, your mind, and therefore your responsibility to be aware of the options available to you. Please familiarise yourself with the potential benefits and dangers of any given healing approach. You may need to select one mode or use various modes in combination to optimise your health. Wisdom based on knowledge will lead you towards the insights you need to assure your own well-being. I suggest considering Reiki as an important element in your mental and physical health programme. Learning about the history and principles of Reiki is one small step towards a greater understanding of the healing modalities available.

### Reiki History

The modern history of Reiki begins with Dr. Mikao Usui (1865-1926). Dr. Usui is said to have travelled through many countries searching for techniques to heal people, body and soul. Finally, he sat down on Mt. Kurama in Japan for a 21 day fasting meditation called "kushu shinren." It was during this purification process that he envisioned the techniques and symbols of energy healing that he named Reiki. He proceeded to travel around Japan healing people and training new students of Reiki.

Usui relied on intuition to know where and when to place his hands and how to conduct healings. One of his students, Dr. Chujiro Hayashi, is credited for adding the specific hand positions that have become standard Reiki procedures. These teachings travelled to Hawaii with Mrs. Hawayo Takata, the first female Reiki master, who trained many Reiki masters in her life time, substantially spreading Reiki in the Western world. She also trained her granddaughter Phyllis Lei Furumoto to perpetuate her Reiki lineage. Reiki techniques and principles have been handed down from teacher to student for nearly a hundred years. During this time, many different styles, techniques and theories have evolved. For a more comprehensive history of Reiki, see Diane Stein's "Essential Reiki."

Originally, Dr. Usui taught Reiki as a gradual progression based on each student's progress as a healer. Later, three distinct levels of Reiki were established. In addition, you may have heard of various healing modes such as Karuna Reiki, Healing Hands, Psychic Reiki, Joh Rei and Pranic healing. All of these healing approaches employ universal energy. Variations occur in terms of history, principles and techniques. Some schools divide Reiki into additional levels or include more symbols or prayers. Be wary of innovations that might be marketing techniques more than healing techniques. Is one better than the other? Some practitioners may claim their system is the original or most effective one. Others argue that if something is already infinite and universal, how can it be made greater?

Whatever claims you encounter, it's truly necessary to experience the energy for yourself. In my own teaching, I focus on the basic concept of Reiki as universal energy. The other techniques that I discuss throughout this book are supplements to Reiki and are offered to help you develop your health holistically. See what works best for you. You might want to begin by receiving a few Reiki healings. If you are impressed by the experience, you can seek a Reiki Master who can train you and attune you to Reiki.

### The Reiki Attunement

Students work with a qualified Reiki Master to receive attunement to Reiki. The Reiki Master invokes the spirit and power of Reiki and draws it into the student. Initiation into Reiki is a powerful experience for both teacher and student. The process requires about ten minutes, followed by a silent self-healing done by the student to allow the energy to flow throughout the body. For some people, the attunement brings great serenity, for others, it brings tears. Admittedly, some people also experience temporary headaches as the energy struggles to clear blocked paths through their minds. In every case, the energy is intense and potentially life-changing. Numerous generations of teachers have handed down the energy and traditions first elaborated by Dr. Usui.

Traditionally, a Reiki Master conducted four attunements to introduce students to level one Reiki. Contemporary authors such as Diane Stein have suggested that just one attunement can be done, in as little as a few minutes, to complete the attunement process. I have used both approaches over the years and finally settled on using the four attunement approach because it gives each student my dedicated energy, intention and attention rather than an assembly line approach. This dedicated time provides an opportunity to discuss a student's goals, hopes and barriers in a highly energetic, heart to heart conversation.

## Is Reiki a Religion?

"Is Reiki a new age religion?" Christians, Buddhists, Muslims and atheists all ask this same basic question. Reiki is not a religion; it's not an opinion or a belief; Reiki is energy. It's a practice as real as swimming is to water, as true as breathing is to air. Reiki is a practice like Yoga, Taiji or meditation that helps you tune into the deep nature of the universe. It's perfectly consistent with any religious or spiritual practice. Reiki requires attunement to higher energies that are present in all things; water, sun, air and every thought. It's not necessary to "believe" in Reiki or "pray" to Reiki, because Reiki doesn't tell you to believe in anything or believe in any God.

> **Rodrigo**
>
> Eight year old Rodrigo was a very agitated, talkative boy from a broken home. Ada, the guardian of the children's home where he lived, reported that he often acted out his anger. During his Reiki session, he fell into a deep sleep, fidgeting in his dreams. After the healing, he continued to sleep for an additional hour. When he finally awoke, he told Ada in Spanish, "it felt like the hands of Jesus on my face." This was a very beautiful moment to share with this innocent boy who had suffered deeply beyond his years. Reiki brought him a profound experience of peace.

Using Reiki means becoming aware and tuning into the energy of the universe. It means to open your heart and mind to new experiences and welcome a new understanding of life. Reiki, like Hinduism, Judaism, Buddhism, Christianity and Islam, stirs compassion and nurtures your deeper appreciation of life. It encourages love and awareness of higher reality. For some, that means an awareness of God. It depends on YOUR path.

Reiki never pushes or commands; it simply supports and encourages you to be the healthiest, wisest, warmest person that you can be. In the last five years, I've attuned Buddhists from Thailand; Christians from India, Sri Lanka, Germany, Holland and the United States; Hindus from India; Muslims from Malaysia and Thailand; Jewish students from Brazil; and non-denominational students from all over the world. Reiki works with everybody!

I would like to share a story with you that took place during one of our recent classes. Gena wrote,

> We began the third day of class with the final initiation of Reiki 1. The meditation was an hour and 45 minutes, with four of us receiving the attunement. I kept my eyes closed and prayed for the power of the Holy Spirit to make known to me how to do Christ's work in the world. I shifted my prayer to Christ, asking Him to show me how He would have me use the healing touch of Reiki in my ministry.
>
> A vision of Christ came to me at this moment. Jesus was wearing all white, and He was moving about slowly on rocky, dusty terrain, coming toward me on a path. I was simply watching Him move along the path with children all about Him. He was moving among them, touching them and touching adults who came near Him too. He kept moving forward, healing

unconditionally. The message I received was to keep moving, touching people as they needed to be healed.

After the session, Tom shared with me that he had invited Jesus into the prayer of my Reiki attunement, consistent with my tradition and beliefs. My vision of Christ at this time, not knowing of Tom's prayer beforehand, is a validation that the universal spirit of energy is the Spirit of Christ and that the healing energy given to me is the healing light of Christ.

After the attunements, each student shared their experience with the group. Jem asked me several times if I had opened the curtains because she had seen a bright white light while she was meditating. No, I had not opened the curtains at all. Then, what was the bright light? Was it the same light that Gena experienced in her vision?

**What is the Source of Reiki?**

The concept of energy may be unfamiliar to you even though civilisations around the world have known about it for thousands of years. The ancient Chinese developed energy disciplines such as Taiji and Qigong that involve moving meditation practices to harness inner energy and universal energy. Spiritual and healing disciplines such as Kundalini and Pranayama date back thousands of years in ancient India. Indian Yogic practice involves control and movement of Prana or life force energy through the body. Similarly, ancient Tibetan monks practised healing that some authors consider to be the original source of the modern system of Reiki. Reiki can be referred to as natural energy, universal energy, cosmic energy or life force, among various other names. When we expand our awareness, consciousness and concepts of nature, the practice and principles of Reiki become superbly simple. I can try to explain a little bit about quantum physics and show that Reiki is consistent with quantum theory, if that helps a little bit.

## Quantum Physics and Reiki

The most intriguing thing that I find about quantum physics is that thought influences matter. All consciousness and all matter are connected in ways that baffle the imagination. Ample scientific experiments confirm that consciousness influences matter and that people can communicate through consciousness at a distance. Although the channel of communication has not yet been established, the results of communication prove that a transfer of information takes place. To the dismay of Einstein himself, the transfer of information takes place faster than the speed of light. Considering the essential oneness of the universe, instantaneous communication comes as no surprise.

Scientific research in the last hundred years has identified deep energy that exists within particles at the quantum level. Every thought, every feeling, all matter and all consciousness are forms of energy. The human mind has the power to control and direct this energy. Interestingly, this causes a challenge for physicists when they observe and measure quantum activity. The moment quantum activity is observed, it is influenced by consciousness. So, "purely objective science" has been proven to be totally impossible.

Another weird thing that physicists have discovered is that atoms are almost completely empty. Atomic physics has shown that solid matter does not really exist. It's just our perception of solid substance that is generated in the mind. Atoms are 99.9999999 percent empty space no matter how solid they may seem.

I hate to tell you this, but this also means that all of the atoms that stick together to make you and me are pretty much empty. Understanding this phenomenon becomes important to the Reiki healer because we realise that we are not really healing a "body" as much as healing consciousness that seems to "inhabit" empty space. In "The Tao of Physics," Fritjof Capra explains that "mass is nothing but a form of energy… and is no longer associated with a material substance and hence particles are not seen as consisting of any basic "stuff" but as bundles of energy."

During a Reiki healing session, energy is transferred from healer to patient. For example, by focusing on a patient who is experiencing sadness or guilt, Reiki balances and transforms negative, unhealthy life situations; this is what we call healing. This parallels findings in quantum physics that show how an observer of quantum physics always influences the outcome of the experiment. For example, if you look for particles, you'll find particles; but if you're looking for waves, you'll find waves. In both Reiki and quantum physics, the mind, thoughts, compassion and intention of the practitioner influence the outcome.

As Dean Radin explains, "in classical physics, objects are regarded as objectively real and independent of the observer. In the quantum world, this is no longer the case." Both allopathic medicine and classical physics are obsessed with objectivity. These approaches consider the patient or particle as an "object" to be treated or as an equation to be measured. In holistic healing approaches such as Reiki, the patient, healer and energy are perceived as a whole, working together as a team for optimum results. Of course the healer influences the healing; of course the patient influences the healing. The universe will have it no other way!

As a society, we privilege science to prove or disprove, proclaim what is real or not real, possible or impossible. By granting this privilege to science, we perpetuate blind obedience to scientific declarations that claim objectivity is good and subjectivity is bad. Unfortunately, orthodox, empirical science can be blind to its own limitations in pursuit of "pure, rational science." Such a perspective, while effective in some fields, also qualifies as "pure, narrow limitation." We might even call this approach "materialist fundamentalism." Is that what your friend means when he claims to be "rational?"

Why do we so often defer to science rather than trust personal intuition and experience? Empirical, objective science may be great for certain geological matters, but in the human realm, it may contribute to personal disempowerment. It makes as much sense to defer to scientists to explain the meta-physical world as it does to allow the government to set standards of honesty.

For centuries, scientists and the general population have believed in a set of natural laws, gravity, linear causation and rational thought. Quantum physics comes along in the early 1900s and informs us that a photon can be in two places at the same time. We learn that a photon can be either a wave or a particle, depending on the observer's expectations and system of measurement. We also learn that space and time are relative perceptions rather than absolute measurements. All protons are linked together throughout the universe. Experiments have proven that probing one proton affects an intertwined proton anywhere in the universe. These innovations in physics have ignited advances in other realms of human thought. We are no longer earth-bound to our little mechanical bodies. The essence of our being is much greater than that.

Quantum physics is every bit as revolutionary, and disturbing to our understanding of ourselves and the universe, as the Copernican Revolution 500 years ago that presented a radically different world view shifting away from an Earth-centred cosmology. Similarly, as you progress in your Reiki and meditation practice, you discover amazing perspectives of life. All things in the universe are one. We are all connected, like one being with billions of fingers, all part of one universal mind; one collective consciousness.

"So, what does all this science have to do with me?" When thoughts of "me" and "I" intrude, we are severed from the unity of life. This egotistical perspective damages our holistic experience of life and perpetuates our industrialised feelings of alienation. Our modern society is painfully out of time and out of tune with nature, as if we were objectively separate from nature.

As environmentalist Joanna Macy describes in "World as Lover, World as Self," the human body is more like the surface of a pond constantly interfacing with the natural world, rather than a being isolated within the confines of our skin. Reducing the ego and relaxing the "I" perspective empower a person to become whole in universal awareness and connectedness. This reduces alienation and leads to awareness described in Buddhism as Anatta, the impersonal non-self.

The mind/universe has a capacity far beyond narrow linear perception. Perceiving and experiencing life holistically opens up vastly different dimensions. We learn to see that our beliefs and patterns of thought severely limit us. Our human brains and consciousness are trapped in old, rational thought. It's like our minds are using computer software written in the seventeenth century while trying to understand phenomena occurring in the twenty first century.

---

**Kirlian Photography**

In the 1960s, Russian researchers discovered energy fields around all living things. They named it "Bio-plasmic energy." Through the use of Kirlian photography, they were effectively able to observe the energy field of any living thing. Soviet scientists made extensive progress with photographic evidence of the energy inherent in all living entities. You might be interested in researching more about Kirlian photography to understand the claims and criticisms of the process.

---

## Conclusion

OK, so don't worry too much if quantum physics boggles your mind. Just because we understand that atoms are not solid, time and space are relative and everything is entangled with everything else, you still need to get up tomorrow morning, eat breakfast and go to work. So, life goes on.

At the same time, we gain awareness that nothing is quite what it seems. We have the ability to overcome limits to our thoughts and consciousness. You might want to read further into quantum physics, but I suggest that your time might be used more effectively meditating in non-discursive thought than trying to disentangle the mysteries of the sub-atomic universe.

Rest assured, Reiki works just as well whether you understand quantum physics or not! You do not need to privilege the scientists, physicists or doctors to figure out if Reiki is real or not. It would be much more valuable to simply receive a healing and discover it for yourself. If you are favourably impressed by the results from your healing session, it may be time to join a Reiki course.

# Chapter Two

# Becoming a Reiki Channel

"Can I become a Reiki healer? Do I need some special gift?" Anybody can be attuned to Reiki and learn to heal. No special gifts are required and you don't need to be psychic. All it truly requires is openness to receive Reiki and discipline to practise. It's important to find a good Reiki master with whom you are comfortable and who feels energetically in tune with you.

I remember the first time that Anchalee sat down in our Reiki room and asked with a look of serious consternation on her face, "Do I have to be a Vegan to do Reiki?" Although I always recommend improvement in diet, there are no strict rules about what you must or must not eat to practise Reiki. Rather, it is helpful to cleanse your body and mind as much as you can prior to Reiki training. To prepare yourself for initiation as a Reiki healer, I suggest observing several steps before receiving your attunement. First, do not drink any alcohol for at least a week. This will help your body detoxify, especially your liver. Second, try to cut down eating meat as much as possible. If you like, abstain from meat completely and give your stomach and intestines a much needed holiday. If you are a smoker, now might be a good time to cut down or refrain from any smoking. If that is asking too much, I understand, but please give it some thought. Finally, I suggest that you practise meditation, Yoga or deep relaxation every day. Taking these steps is indicative of your commitment and willingness to personally transform yourself through Reiki. No, I cannot prescribe a specific behaviour that you must or must not do. All I can do is make suggestions that will prepare you for the powerful energetic experience that Reiki generates.

## Reiki Principles

Dr. Usui recommended daily meditation to his Reiki students plus observance of the following five principles. While the principles taught by Dr. Usui may seem quite basic, it is important to approach them with greater commitment as you progress in your Reiki training. This section describes and interprets the Reiki principles for your benefit. It guides you in knowing how to incorporate the principles into your personal transformation.

### Today, I give thanks for my many blessings

Simple as this principle sounds, it does indeed require practice. Saying grace before meals, bowing to Buddhist, Hindu or Christian images and praying before bedtime are all important expressions of gratitude. Another approach is to write down all the things in your life for which you are grateful. Meditate on these and see for yourself the amazing abundance you have been provided. Finally, meditate on the words and feelings of "thank you" and "gratitude." At the same time, honour your parents, teachers and elders. This can be done through the Buddhist practice of "sharing merit" which involves sharing loving kindness and compassion to all beings at the conclusion of each meditation session. Do you know the power of grateful consciousness?

Japanese researcher Masaru Emoto experimented with the effects of consciousness on water. One experiment in his book "The Message from Water" involved writing the words "thank you" and "love, appreciation" on pieces of paper that were attached to water samples. The water was then frozen and photographed through a microscope. The resultant photographs showed elegant crystal structures of balance and integrity. In contrast, the same experiment was conducted with the words, "You make me sick. I will kill you." The photographs of these crystals were distorted, dispersed and clearly unhealthy. These experiments show that water responds to human language and consciousness.

The experiments with water yield physical representation of the importance of gratitude in our daily lives and in our practice of Reiki. Imagine the influence that your thoughts and words have on a larger scale. Review Emoto's research and photos for yourself to see his spectacular findings. The photographs of crystals may also provide you with a strong visual understanding of quantum physics. Then, you can judge for yourself the power of consciousness and its influence on physical matter.

## Today, I will not worry

Don't worry! Easier said then done. To arrest anxiety requires strong mindfulness during the process of worrying. Observe the movement of your thoughts carefully during your meditation and mindfulness practice. Each time a worry arises, identify it and understand its nature. Be kind to your worries; don't chase them away, deny or suppress them. Rather, seek to understand the nature of your worries and how they influence you. Your worries exist in your mind for some purpose.

At one time, your worries may have served you very well in terms of security or identity. The question remains, are your worries serving your best interests, or are they hangovers from an earlier time in your life? Watch your worries and discern which ones are redundant and which ones are beneficial to your well being. Determine if your worries are your own, or if you may have inherited them from your culture or family. Mindfulness practice supports you to know your worries well without falling prey to them.

**Today, I will not be angry**

This principle of Reiki is also quite easy, as long as everything is going well. Be mindful any time that you feel anger arising in your heart. Watch it like you would keep your eyes on a mean dog; be kind to it, don't turn your back on it and don't threaten it, but be very alert to its danger. With true understanding, anger and fear no longer need to exist. Ultimately, catch your anger arising before it converts into words; disarm it before it becomes full-blown action. True understanding penetrates to the root of every cause.

Anger indicates some deeper aspect of your perspective of life. It may be rooted in righteous indignation, unrecognised fear or banal prejudice. Observe and understand the politics of your anger. Decide for yourself if these are an essential part of your being, valuable feelings by which to know the truth of your soul, or dangerous automatic reactions that are sabotaging your peacefulness. Mindfulness through meditation will greatly assist you in this process.

The venerable Zen Buddhist monk, Thich Nhat Hanh, describes how to recognise irritation with a few attentive breaths to transform it into something more positive such as understanding or love. He explains that anger and worry are destructive energies. Whether you are talking about science or spirituality, energy cannot be destroyed. All you can do is convert it into something more constructive. Forgiveness, like love, is a constructive energy.

When you find yourself angry, this is a beacon telling you to learn how to forgive. You can hold on to your anger if you choose, based on the rationale that anger is as natural as anything else. Indeed, anger, fear, resentment and jealousy naturally exist within all of us. The work of meditation is to generate keen awareness of all feelings. With mindfulness, you generate fine awareness of all feelings, not just the nasty ones. The difference is that positive feelings are healthy and nutritious, whereas negative feelings are destructive. Wholeness comes when you work with all aspects of yourself, transforming destructive energies into something positive by looking deeply into the nature of your feelings and overcoming ignorance.

### Learning Situations

Every situation is a learning situation. There are NO exceptions. The lessons of life repeat over and over until you learn, and then the lessons are no longer necessary. You can then move forward in your development.

## Today, I will do my work honestly

How can you deepen your commitment to this principle? Observe yourself throughout the day to be sure you are acting, speaking and thinking honestly. Continue the observation until you discover any wayward actions or thoughts that fall short of honesty. That is, be honest with yourself anytime you discover a sense of dishonesty. Then, work with yourself and find ways to purify your thoughts before those thoughts transform into dishonest words or actions.

Discussing the Sutras of Patanjali in "The 8 Limbs of Yoga," Bhava Ram writes, "If we firmly establish ourselves in truth, we no longer need worry about sustaining deceptions... We move further from ignorance and closer to the Divine." One way to test your own honesty is to observe yourself next time you are criticising a friend. Catch yourself before criticism leaks from your mouth by reminding yourself, "he may have his weaknesses and flaws, but first, what are my own weaknesses and flaws?" Pausing to ask this question stimulates mindfulness, self-awareness and honesty with self. It also helps you be more compassionate with your friends.

Similarly, next time you are complaining about government officials, ask yourself, "In what way do I personally contribute to lying and corruption in government?" This is a tricky question. One, it disarms criticism and exchanges it for a personal mirror. It challenges you to check yourself before blaming another. Once you have reviewed your own honesty and integrity, proceed to mindfully evaluate the objects of criticism.

## Today, I will be kind to my neighbours and every living thing

The fifth principle of Reiki challenges you to open your heart further, to find a kind word and smile for those around you. Speak gently and be mindful of the effects of your words on others. This principle supports you to consider your diet and whether or not you are living a non-violent life. Eating meat or animal products that are derived from the death or suffering of animals goes against the spiritual practice of kindness and compassion. Look carefully at your diet and see what needs to be removed immediately and what needs to be gradually reduced.

Describing the Yoga principle of Ahimsa, Swami Kriyananda writes, "it is important to understand that the life flowing in our veins is the same life which flows in the veins of all creatures." It might be too shocking to become a Vegan overnight, but it remains incumbent on a Reiki healer to consider taking peaceful steps in that direction. Taking Vegan steps shows kindness towards each animal that you restrain from killing and eating. It also shows kindness towards self by eating food that is optimally suited for human digestion.

One by one, remove items from your diet that fail the principle of kindness. Further along, reduce or eliminate animal products such as milk, eggs and leather as you completely embody kindness at optimum levels. More ideas concerning Veganism to support your Reiki practice are discussed in chapter eight.

**Benefits of Reiki**

"What are the benefits of Reiki?" Straight from the beginning, Reiki will help you relax. If nothing more and nothing less, you can use Reiki to relieve stress. This is of great importance because stress causes headaches, migraines, ulcers and a thousand other physical maladies. So, the sooner you apply Reiki, the sooner you can calm your mind and heal psychological pain. As you get deeper into Reiki practice, other benefits will accrue. Reiki will cleanse, open and unite all levels of your being (body, mind and soul). This will help you feel more whole, more complete and more in tune with yourself.

If you decide to study Reiki and do healings for yourself and others, additional benefits will manifest. Your sensitivity and insight will increase as you heal more people. You will also experience an increase in your consciousness and energy level. Week by week, you will develop spiritual awareness and appreciation. This is not a guarantee as much as a description of the most common experiences that students encounter during their training and practice. Within a short time, you will gain clearer intuition and understanding of yourself and others. Taken together, these experiences will boost your confidence and your ability to help others.

## Is Reiki Safe?

"I always read about the benefits of Reiki, but is it really safe?" This question comes up quite often. Most sources claim that Reiki is totally and perfectly safe. I would like to agree, except that some issues remind us that we must be very careful when healing and working in the spiritual realm. For example, some people are afraid of ghosts and are particularly wary of something like Reiki because they can feel it but can't see or explain it. Very sensitive people unknowingly or unconsciously absorb negative energy from people, spirits or the environment that can adversely affect them.

Reiki itself is not dangerous. The most likely danger to occur during a Reiki session is that a healer picks up negative energy or feelings from a patient. I've seen healers crying, feeling depressed and experiencing heavy tension in their hands while giving Reiki. It's important to remember that the purpose of healing is to raise a patient's level of energy and remove unwanted energy/emotions from their hearts. This does not imply that the healer should take on those energies.

Many students mention that they pick up negative energy even when they are just walking down the street or in a crowded bus. For example, Ashta felt very susceptible to negative energy in her workplace. During her healing session, she asked, "What can I do for psychic protection?" First, we can ask why those negative energies were being directed at her. Was it something she did that needs to be addressed through direct communication? Was she attracting psychic attacks for some hidden reason? Later, she asked, "How can I open my heart?" This becomes very complex because if she establishes psychic protection, it might seem that she is closing herself off from the universe, just the opposite of opening her heart. I suggested that she send compassion to the person that seemed to be attacking her. This raises the issues of openness, susceptibility and vulnerability.

How can we know how open we should be to the world? A healer needs to be open to the flow of energy. This includes coming into contact with negative emotions or psychic attachments. If you are susceptible to picking up unwanted emotions from others, look into your heart and determine why you are tuning into those feelings. Are you seeking reflection or confirmation through the feelings of others? It seems normal to gravitate towards people who emanate positive feelings that resonate with us, but what about negative feelings? Do negative or stressful feelings from a crowded airport resonate with feelings hidden within your shadow self? Reflect on these types of situations to help understand your unconscious self.

Do we need to be vulnerable as healers? Yes, in the same way that by opening our hearts to love, we need to accept vulnerability. As Tennyson wrote, "Tis better to have loved and lost than to have never loved at all." So, the answer is yes, you are vulnerable while healing, but that does not mean that you set yourself up as prey to all energy that lurks in dark shadows. The important thing is to be aware of energies and emotions whether they are positive, negative or undefined. Remain open to energy of any sort, but that does not mean you should absorb those energies. Be aware, and make a conscious, informed decision of which energies are conducive to your well being and to the promotion of your patient's well being. In correspondence with one of my students, we discussed these issues:

Hi Tom,

I have been using Reiki recently to heal my brother and a good friend, both of whom have big emotional issues that I helped them clear, but in the process, I picked up some of their problems accidentally. I learned that when we send Reiki, it is supposed to be channelled through us and we are not supposed to pick up any of their problems so I'm not sure why this is happening. I know I am psychically quite attached to both of them so maybe this is the problem. For example, when my brother has a sleepless night with worry, I often have a sleepless night for no apparent reason, and I only discover later that he didn't sleep that same night.

Anne

Dear Anne,

For now, concentrate on doing healings only for yourself until you are very strong and certain that you are ready to be of service to others. Are you doing regular self healing? Do this every day for at least half an hour to remove any unwanted stress or energies. Work on each chakra and sweep your hands through your aura to cleanse it. Create a "cocoon" of Reiki around yourself. Visualise Reiki symbols and white light all around you. This will purify and release any energy attachments.

Yes, your psychic attachment to your brother and friend is causing some distress. Try to detach from the healing process. See yourself as a witness to the Reiki flowing through you for the benefit of others. Request Reiki and thank Reiki. Be aware of your expectations because this can also be a form of attachment. Be sure that you are sending energy and not receiving energy while healing; receive energy only inasmuch as you need to know what is taking place, but not so much as to harm you. Hope this helps.

Sincerely,

Tom

Many students are living completely in their minds, and are relatively disconnected from their hearts and bodies. In terms of energy, this means that all of their energy is up in their brains, leaving them unbalanced and poorly grounded. In these cases, I explain how to move the sense of "self" from the head to the heart to understand how you feel, rather than what you think about your situation.

What does it mean to move myself to my heart? Moving the self means to shift your consciousness or re-locate your awareness. It means moving the sense of "I" from the head down to the heart. In cerebral consciousness, the sense of self is in the brain. Relatively speaking, breathing through the nose seems to take place below your centre of awareness. When you move your sense of self down to your heart (cardiac consciousness), it will seem that breathing takes place above your centre of awareness. This technique facilitates a deeper understanding of self and a broader awareness of relationships from a heart-felt perspective.

In summary, Reiki is very safe, but it is also wise to take precautions. In a similar paradox, keep your heart open while monitoring what passes through it. I would like to suggest a few techniques that you can practise to supplement your Reiki experience.

These rituals focus your mind. At the same time, your intention empowers the rituals.

- Always request Reiki to purify and protect you while healing
- Use incense or candles to purify your healing or work environment
- Practise meditation regularly; this raises the energy level in your mind as well as your environment
- Practise feelings of equanimity with all experiences and feelings; be equanimous with pleasure as much as pain; with relaxation as much as stress
- Send loving kindness to friends, family, strangers and enemies with equal compassion
- When you truly feel threatened and require security from psychic attack, cross your arms, cross your feet and mentally surround yourself in a cocoon of pure white light

### Meditation for Reiki

Reiki training begins with meditation. My students and I always sit in a circle together. Sometimes we meditate in silence; other times, we use a guided chakra meditation as described in chapter four. Meditation is an essential aspect of spiritual and personal growth because it calms the mind and opens the channels for energy to flow freely through you. Meditation deepens mindfulness, which is essential during both the healing process and in your daily experience of life. As a healer, it's important to be aware of what patients are feeling energetically, emotionally and physically. You need to be tuned into the person moment by moment so you can effectively support them and guide them through the healing process.

Please take note: Meditation is not just concentration! Everywhere I travel, I meet people young and old who claim they cannot meditate. The truth is, they cannot concentrate, and they mistakenly consider this to be a failure. Meditation involves much more than concentration. Mindfulness (bare attention) is a vital method for knowing your deep self, recognising your true feelings and thoughts as they occur, for gaining awareness of your strengths and weaknesses, biases and fears. By being aware of all these aspects of self, you gain control over them. You will no longer be controlled by thoughts and feelings that constantly occur, automatically and subconsciously in your mind.

By knowing yourself, you learn to release your attachment to that self. This release allows the energy of the universe to flow unhindered by the limitations and illusions of your human ego. The purpose of meditation is to be aware of the wandering of the mind and to bring it back to a point of focus. A great benefit of training in this level of awareness is psychological healing. Depression can effectively be treated with this technique as described in "Mindfulness Based Cognitive Therapy for Depression" by Segal, Williams and Teasdale.

It is helpful to meditate before any Reiki training, healing or distance healing. The basic meditation technique involves observing your breathing at the nostrils or at the abdomen, whichever seems most suitable for you. Carefully observe the sensation of inhaling, observe a pause, and follow the complete exhalation. Any time you are distracted from your focus by thoughts or feelings, simply bring your attention back to the breathing process, your anchor in the here and now. This process allows you to observe thoughts and emotions without getting involved in them. It also heightens your awareness of physical sensations and the flow of energy throughout the body. In "Cutting through Spiritual Materialism," Chogyam Trungpa explains that,

> In the practice of meditation we neither encourage emotions nor suppress them. By seeing them clearly, by allowing them to be as they are, we no longer permit them to serve as a means of entertaining and distracting us... Meditation involves seeing the transparency of concepts... not just concentrating on one particular point, but including the entire situation of life.

Trungpa also warns us to be careful because the practice of concentration can reinforce the ego. Remember, mindfulness does not mean concentration. Mindfulness is based on the present moment, not seeking particular results or levels of awakening, which would be the goals of the ego. Just be in the moment; observe it and experience it as it occurs. Finally, he writes that, "whenever we have a dualistic notion such as, 'I am doing this because I want to achieve a particular state of consciousness'... then automatically we separate ourselves from the reality of what we are." With these parameters in mind, I would like to suggest a few basic steps to help tune your mindfulness to the present moment. Further meditation techniques are explained in later chapters.

- Begin by sitting 20 minutes per session
- Observe the breath as it passes through the nostrils or observe the rising and falling of your abdomen with each breath
- When your mind wanders, bring it back to observing the breath
- Mentally scan your body from head to foot, from foot to head (body scan)
- Observe all sensations without attachment, without analysis
- Maintain attention on your breathing
- Be aware of each thought that arises, without attachment

Meditation helps us penetrate the neurotic thought pattern that is the fringe of the ego. In the practice of meditation, Trungpa explains that all thoughts are the same: pious thoughts, beautiful thoughts, religious or calm thoughts are still all thoughts. The point is not merely to cultivate calm thoughts and suppress so-called neurotic thoughts. Nevertheless, being so mundanely human, we are very busy attempting to rid ourselves of irritation. We are constantly seeking distractions from ourselves. As a result, we fail to look into the raw material of daily life that we experience right here inside of us. The point of meditation is getting beyond the words, techniques, and ideas, and diving into what we truly are.

Yeah, so, meditation is tricky! I would like to summarise some of the seeming paradoxes of meditation as gleaned through my own experience and dozens of books on the subject:

Begin by focusing on the breath. Become aware of the subtleties of the breath, mindful of distractions and mental discourse, but not merely concentration. Calm the mind enough to see clearly, but not simply to achieve calmness. Meditate to generate piercing insight into the true nature of things without attaching to this accomplishment. Become aware of a perspective from beyond the "I" who meditates. Transcend the separation between the one meditating and the breath being observed; don't establish that duality in the first place. Try to recognise that "breathing is breathing" or "the universe is breathing," rather than me and my ego are breathing.

Towards the end of your meditation session, send loving kindness to all beings. Be aware that you are not really "sending" because all of us are already one. Meditation leads to "being the compassion." Maintain mindfulness of the breath as a tool of focus, without attachment to the tool and without attaching to concentration. Just be in the moment without mental discourse. Be aware of feelings and thoughts as they come and go. Be.

## Conclusion

This chapter has discussed a lot of ideas directly related to Reiki and other concepts such as quantum physics and meditation that can supplement your understanding and appreciation of Reiki. Of course, no amount of explanation is capable of substituting for your personal experience of Reiki energy. Receiving Reiki from a healer will amplify your personal insight into Reiki exponentially. In fact, many people come to my clinic not to study or get healed, but to learn for themselves what Reiki is all about and how it resonates with them.

The response is often an emphatic "Wow!" although some people don't really notice any sensations at all during the process.

The only way to know is to try it yourself. Neither those who believe nor confirmed sceptics can say with any certainty what the nature of Reiki is like until having received the energy. Oddly enough, even after many healings, you may still be at a loss for words to explain how Reiki feels to you. This leads us to chapter three where I explain the techniques that are generally covered in Reiki 1 training.

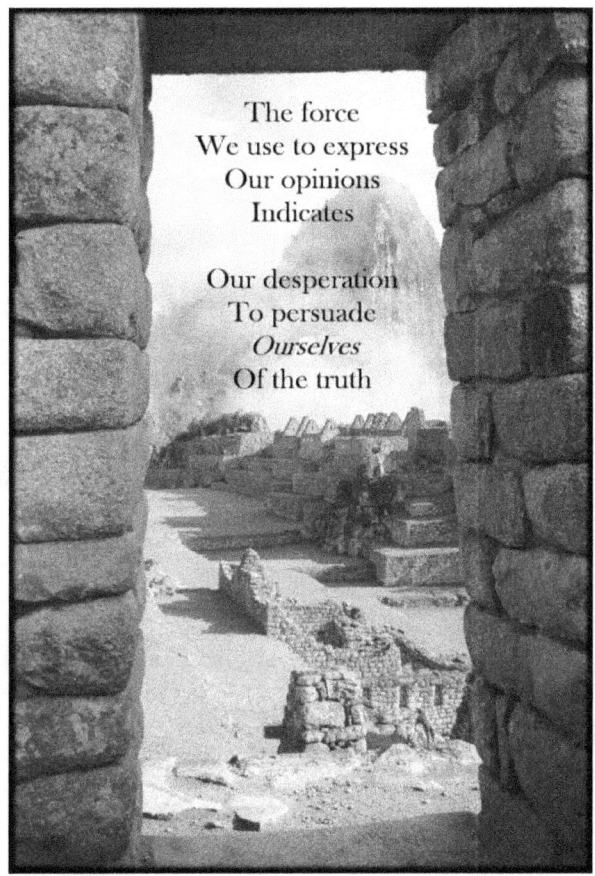

The force
We use to express
Our opinions
Indicates

Our desperation
To persuade
*Ourselves*
Of the truth

# Chapter Three

# Training and Healing with Reiki 1

Reiki classes are a lot of fun. We enjoy having a house full of new and old students who come to share their experience and exchange energy. It's always a collegial and very international atmosphere. Many weekends, we have students from three or four different continents, a global gathering of people seeking personal healing and growth. Personal transformation through Reiki is a beautiful experience between you and the universe. Truth is, we spend a lot of time during class sipping tea in between meditations and sharing life experiences. Meanwhile, we practise the technical procedures that are important to Reiki 1. Reiki can be used for healing and purifying self, other people, animals, plants, food, crystals, water and your environment. After your attunement, it's important to practise Reiki regularly on yourself and with other people.

Are you still not sure about all this energy talk? If you are still sceptical or unsure, it might be wise to receive a Reiki treatment before investing the time and money required to study the complete course. Receipt of a Reiki treatment should clarify unequivocally whether or not you wish to proceed to become a Reiki healer. I've talked to people who simply try to prove that energy healing doesn't work, rather than opening up and trying it. What's the point of scepticism for the sake of scepticism? That would be like receiving one of the finest violins ever designed from the great violin maker Antonio Stradivari himself. You place it on your shoulder, draw the bow across the strings and create a deathly screech! Then, you boldly claim, "This thing doesn't work!"

Are you ready to study, get tuned and perform the music of Reiki? The following sections guide you through your healing practice to be sure you include all the essential steps for the well being of you and your patients.

**Self Healing**

"Why do I need to heal myself, I'm not sick!" Sorry if I've given the impression that you must be sick and must need healing. Rather, I mean to say that giving yourself Reiki will balance and strengthen every aspect of your being. It may be true that you are not ill, but that is not equivalent to saying that you wouldn't benefit from further development. Waiting until you are sick to begin any sort of health programme is quite silly, like waiting for a car accident before purchasing auto insurance.

The point with Reiki and other forms of preventative health care is to establish positive habits and discipline to keep yourself happy and healthy, not waiting for illness or depression to take over your life. Through personal transformation, you address all issues in your body, mind and life style before they manifest as illness, pain or infection. This is what we mean by health care rather than illness management. Health care means a lot more than just treating headaches. A good example comes from one student who writes,

> Hello Tom,
>
> As you know I am not very good at writing my feelings but I can tell you Reiki has changed my life a lot. I have the impression it is still changing my life every day.
>
> When we did the initiation you asked me what I most wanted in my life. I told you that I wanted some balance in my life and bit by bit I am achieving it from doing Reiki. At the moment I do Reiki on myself and with people who are very close to me. I have automatically changed some habits. I have stopped smoking without a problem and I have lost interest in drinking alcohol. Also I have changed some eating habits such as not eating anything after 8 pm. All this has happened just because my body asked for it. Also I feel much more balanced in my emotions.
>
> What I most like is that I am learning to be patient and have confidence that things will be alright. Even with the experience of the loss of my sister, I feel that in the end all things are going to be fine and I feel peace inside my body. So Tom I really can't tell you how grateful I am for you introducing me to Reiki.
>
> Greetings,
>
> Nathalie

After studying Reiki, you may be excited to hurry up and begin healing your friends and family. That is very noble; but please begin with a series of self healings. Dedicate 45 to 60 minutes per day to healing yourself, covering every chakra plus your knees and feet. The process for self healing is basically the same as when healing others. Follow the guidelines in the following sections and apply these to yourself. Observe the photos in chapter four to see suitable hand positions for each chakra. Heal yourself thoroughly until your confidence, mindfulness and sensitivity are firm.

After your attunement and training, practise Reiki on yourself every day for at least 21 consecutive days. The 21 day self healing programme symbolises Dr. Usui's 21 day fasting meditation. This practice increases the energy flow through your body, healing any issues that are blocking you. Daily self healing also increases your sensitivity to the energy flowing through your hands. As your confidence and sensitivity increase, you can extend your practice to healing family, friends and animals.

I suggest conducting self healing on some occasions beginning at your head and proceeding down to the feet. Other days, begin at your feet and move your way up to your head. By alternating in this way, you develop a sense for the difference between head-downward and feet-upward healing sessions. Soon, you will intuitively know which pattern works best for you under any given circumstances. Your Reiki and meditation practice will follow its own path. You may encounter some of the phenomena described here plus your own unique experiences. For example, one new student described her Reiki and meditation practice as follows:

Dear Tom,

Since Sunday I've started my meditation and Reiki before bedtime. Although it's only 10 - 15 minutes, I intend to do it everyday and I believe that I can do it longer in the near future. Your voice still echoes in my head during meditation :) My mind still wanders but your voice reminds me to bring it back to my breathing.

For Reiki, I do only 3 chakras each day, and change to another 3 chakras the next day, or repeat the chakra where I feel I most need it. Mostly, I don't feel anything in my body, but I gain peace in my mind. That makes me happy and have better sleep. To me, it's like self-observation. So I take note how I feel each day. Thank you very much. I did try Reiki on my crown chakra and third-eye chakra when I felt stressed, and after that I felt much more relaxed. This week, I did Reiki on my shoulder muscle pain. The pain is still there but Reiki helps to relax it more.

Yours,

Onn

## When to give Reiki

Trust your intuition to know how many healing sessions are required. In some cases, just one healing brings many benefits. For some patients, you may give Reiki three days in a row. For others, give Reiki on alternate days. Most often, I schedule healings once a week so people have sufficient time to absorb the energy and begin making personal changes in their lives that were inspired by Reiki.

Please do not give Reiki to other people when you are ill, angry or upset. Preserve your energy and heal yourself first! Very importantly, never try to give Reiki to somebody who does not want it. Reiki should never be forced; it must be received willingly. With most students, I suggest that they practise healing with family or friends as soon as they can. This gives hands-on experience and feedback to guide them in their practice. One exception to this was a student who was having relationship troubles with her partner. She wanted to heal him right away, but I firmly suggested that she concentrate on healing herself. The reason being, they were struggling with intense mutual expectations. I felt that her expectations of the relationship would get grafted onto her expectations from Reiki. Giving Reiki to her partner might also emphasise her perspective that it was her boyfriend who needed healing and change, and that she did not. I discouraged that perspective. She agreed to this, and for several weeks worked exclusively on self healing and self perception. A couple of months later, she clearly understood the logic of focusing on healing herself.

Does a person's openness determine how much Reiki she or he will receive? The experience of giving and receiving Reiki differs for every person. It depends on how ready they are for healing and how open they are to making changes in their lives. If somebody knows they aren't ready, they will simply tell you not to give them Reiki. If a person agrees to receive healing, but it seems like they aren't receiving energy, this suggests they aren't quite ready to receive at a deeper level of their being. In this case, discuss the situation and ask them to verbalise their willingness to open, receive and heal.

## Giving Reiki

Now it's time to study the processes used when giving Reiki. This section is based on the assumption that you are really ready to work with a Reiki master and apply these instructions in your practice. If you still have never received Reiki or been attuned to Reiki, your ability to perform the procedures in the rest of this chapter may be rather limited. On the other hand, you may find that you command sufficient energy to employ the techniques in this chapter to perform healings. I remember when Yod came to study Reiki the first time; he described many personal encounters where friends could feel his energy even though he had not yet been trained as a healer. In Yod's case, he already had high energy that seemed to switch on instinctively whenever his family or friends were feeling down. For most people, your energy may not be strong enough and you won't be able to sense anything. This might make you feel disappointed that these techniques don't work. Please don't sell yourself short; find a Reiki Master to attune and train you. I promise you that these techniques work; they are real. All it takes is training and practice.

The first thing to do is clean the area where you provide Reiki. Creating a clean and fresh atmosphere is important to establishing a favourable impression on your patient. At the same time, the cleaning of the area can serve as a ritual for calming your own mind prior to healing. Clean your hands and drink some water before healing because the flow of energy tends to dehydrate people.

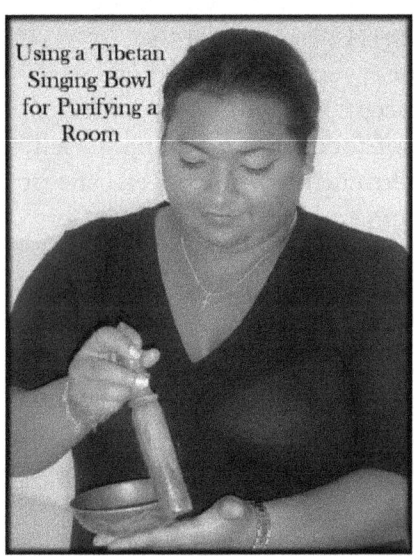

Using a Tibetan Singing Bowl for Purifying a Room

I suggest that you meditate in your healing room prior to your patient's arrival. This gives you time to relax your body and mind.

When your patient or friend arrives, discuss the healing process and which issues they would like to address. Confirm that they are really open to receive Reiki. Ask them to lie down on your healing table and make themselves comfortable. Then, request Reiki to provide the healing energy and protect you by invoking a personalised Reiki blessing.

## Blessings

Thought, like Reiki, is a powerful energy. It's essential to develop your thoughts in positive, sacred terms especially for making divine blessings and devotions. Recite a blessing in your heart expressing your intentions each time you begin a healing session. Create your own wording to commence your healing. A sample request for Reiki may be along the following lines, "Reiki, please perform this healing for Pam. Please guide me to do this healing to the best of my ability and for Pam's optimum well-being. Please heal her at the physical, mental and emotional levels of her being. Thank you very much." To this basic request, you can also ask for information that will guide your patient towards better health. Some Christians also request Jesus to be present during the healing. Whatever your personal system of belief, you can weave it into your Reiki blessing.

### Sensing Energy

"Tom, I still don't feel anything!" How many students have written to me worrying that they couldn't feel the energy? They always say they feel relaxed after healing, or have a sense that energy is circulating around their heads, but still insist that they "can't feel anything." If this is your worry, I suggest the following techniques to develop sensitivity in your hands: Practise meditation as described earlier. Bring your hands to your heart as in a prayer position. Touch the tips of your middle fingers lightly together. Deeply inhale and exhale several times. Focus your attention on the sensations in your hands. This is the meditation technique recommended by Dr. Usui called "ghasso." As you gain sensitivity, increase the distance between your palms and observe the flow of energy.

To practise sensing energy in another way, continue meditating. Put full attention to your right index finger and point it at your left palm. From 5 centimetres (2 inches) away, draw patterns with your index finger and observe the sensations on your left palm. Practise for about 5 minutes. Then, reverse your hands and repeat for an additional 5 minutes. Your sensitivity and awareness will increase with training. Practise all the techniques in this chapter until you are confident in your own ability.

During your self healing session, experiment with the distance of your hands from your body. In some cases, place your hands directly on your body. In other cases, allow a gap of 5 to 30 centimetres (2 to 12 inches) between your hand and body. Observe the sensations in your palms and fingers to determine the ideal location.

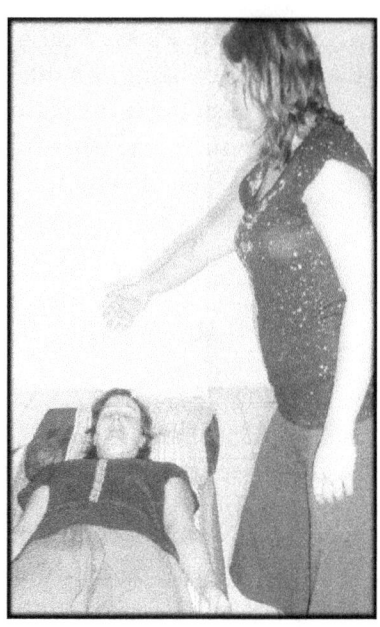

## Sweeping and Scanning

Prepare a comfortable place for your patient to lie on a sofa, bed or on the floor. With your patient lying comfortably on the healing surface, sweep your hands through their aura to get a feeling for their energy. Sweeping clears the entire body of congested or dirty energy and straightens out the aura before and after a healing. To sweep the whole body:

- Relax your wrist and fingers
- Sweep using one hand or both hands, whichever feels most comfortable for you
- Place a smoky quartz or tourmaline crystal about 20 centimetres (8 inches) beyond the patient's feet for grounding
- Begin sweeping from approximately 20 centimetres (8 inches) beyond the patient's crown chakra
- Stand in one position with your feet firmly planted on the ground
- Use a long, continuous movement from above the head to below the feet
- Your hand can be anywhere from 10 to 50 centimetres (4 to 20 inches) from the body

- Practice sweeping both quickly and slowly to determine your optimum pace
- Scan their body to identify the flow or blockage of energy in each layer of their aura
- After you sweep past the feet, shake the energy off your hand three times into the grounding stone

After several sweeps, the sensitivity in your hands should increase. Continue the sweeping motion and increase focus on sensations in your hand. This is the point where you begin scanning, or reading, their energy. As you sweep and scan their aura, observe any sensations of blockage, resistance or heaviness. Sweeping and scanning help you determine if any specific or serious issues need to be addressed during the healing. This also helps you determine if healing should begin at the crown or at the feet. Sweeping can also be applied on a specific location such as an arm or leg in the event that your patient is feeling heaviness or tension in that area.

Apply this same procedure when you are healing yourself. It will probably be easier if you are standing or sitting when you sweep your own aura, rather than lying down. See what works best for you.

When a person is experiencing acute pain, a ridge can be found in their energetic field about 25 to 30 centimetres (10 to 12 inches) away, but sometimes a full metre (3 feet) away! Scan their energy field to sense heat, congestion or tension. Find the ridge and smooth it out. Gradually bring your hand closer and closer to the patient's body until you can touch their skin without them feeling any pain. As you gain more sensitivity with sweeping and scanning, you will be able to diagnose pain more accurately.

**Healing Positions**

Sit or stand so you are stable and can hold a position comfortably for 5 to 10 minutes. Some teachers suggest beginning a healing at the head while others suggest beginning at the feet. Experiment to determine what feels right for each person you heal. Trust your intuition in each situation. Be mindful and honour any thoughts, feelings or instructions that arise during healing. Reiki always goes where it is needed, so relax and let it flow.

The photos in chapter 4 show suitable positions for placing your hands during a healing. Apply Reiki directly to the seven major chakras, plus knees and feet. As you gain experience and knowledge, you will intuitively know the best location to place your hands. Initially, let your hands hover 25 centimetres (12 inches) above the body and gradually get closer. Decide if you will make physical contact at each chakra or stay in the aura a short distance away. At most chakras, you can touch a person's body directly. At private or sensitive areas such as the throat, breasts and genitals, maintain a distance of about 10 centimetres (4 inches). Use common sense along with mutual respect and Reiki will flow optimally. Some healers give Reiki only on the front of the body while others give it both front and back. Trust your intuition to decide where to apply your hands, depending on the time available, symptoms and the setting where you perform the healing.

**Duration of Healing**

Observe the flow of Reiki in your hands. You may feel warmth, tingling, tickling, pulsing, coolness or maybe nothing at all. When the sensations change, this indicates that you can proceed to the next position. If in doubt, remain at each position about 5 minutes. The brow and crown chakras may require more energy and time. Overall, a healing session may take 45 to 90 minutes, depending on the depth of the healing that you intend. For example, if you are at home with your brother who is feeling very stressed and has a sore back, a 90 minute Reiki session covering front and back may be suitable. With children, 1 or 2 minutes per chakra is sufficient; a complete session may require only 10 minutes.

The first time I gave Reiki to a baby was on the beach in Perú. Ahaba was only a year and a half old at the time. She was crabby and restless, so her mother asked me to provide a little Reiki. I placed my hands on her crown and brow for just a few minutes. She was suddenly very quiet with watchful eyes. Shortly after that, she pulled away and played quietly by herself for the remainder of the morning. It's interesting that some scientists dismiss Reiki as merely a placebo or wishful thinking. It's obvious that the last thing that a crying baby wants is some big stranger putting his hands on her head. Ahaba accepted my touch unquestioningly even though she wouldn't sit still for her own mother. Being an infant, she couldn't possibly have held any preconceptions or expectations of what Reiki would do for her.

Some people may not be sceptical but they simply don't know what you're talking about when you mention Reiki to help them with their pain. In cases like these, keep your healing process very simple. If somebody has pain in one specific area, use Reiki directly on that location. If for example you are sitting in the library with a friend who has a headache, applying Reiki at just one or two head positions is sufficient. This should be followed up with a more thorough healing session when you get to a more suitable location. Giving Reiki at just one or two chakras is not meant as a regular practice; regular Reiki sessions should be very thorough, covering all chakras and healing in a holistic, systematic manner.

## Balancing the Chakras

Balancing the chakras after a healing session brings the whole being into tune. Balancing the chakras smoothes out energy excesses or deficiencies. It also balances people between their physical and spiritual selves; between their feeling and thinking selves; between action and communication. Refer to chapter four to confirm the location of each of the chakras. To balance the chakras,

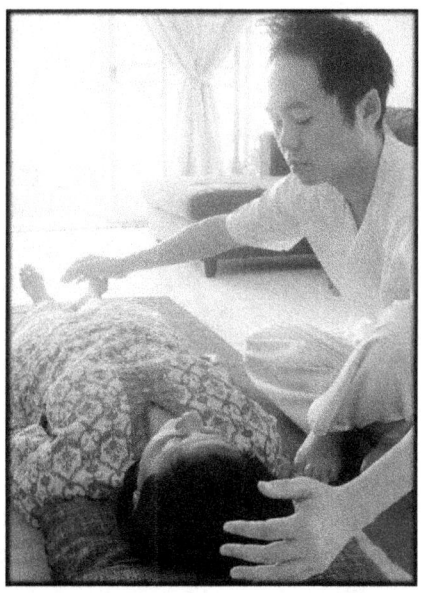

- Place one hand on the crown and your other hand on the root until you feel the energy between the two chakras is balanced. This position brings the physical nature of the first chakra into tune with the spiritual aspects of the crown chakra. Observe the feelings in your hands until the sensations from both hands come into equilibrium. Your hands may automatically move of their own accord when the chakras are properly balanced.

- Hold one hand at the brow chakra and your other hand at the navel chakra until they feel balanced. This position brings the emotions and pleasures of the second chakra into balance with the intellectual and analytical characteristics of the sixth chakra. Be sure to keep your arms and hands relaxed or you may not be able to sense the subtle energies that indicate balance.

- Hold one hand at the throat chakra and one hand at the solar plexus until they feel balanced. Hold this position until both hands experience the same sensations. In some cases, one hand may feel heavier or tenser than the other. This position balances the action orientation of the third chakra with the communicative and creative energies of the fifth chakra.

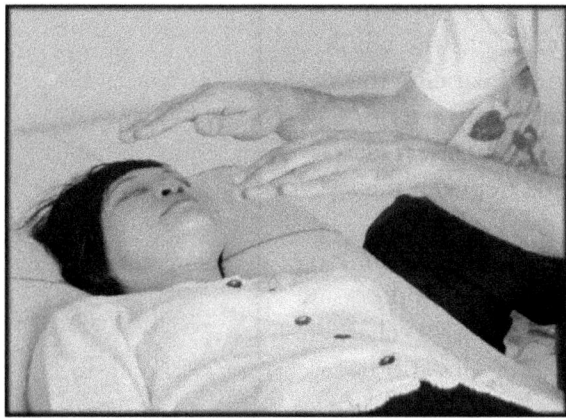

- Bring both hands to the heart chakra until the energy in both hands feels balanced. From this position, I like to lift my hands high like an eagle spreading its wings to open the heart chakra to universal love. The process of opening chakras is explained in more detail in chapter four.

## Closing the Aura

After healing, it's important to clean up the energy around your patient and put everything in order. Closing the aura leaves your patient surrounded by goodness. Relatively speaking, this process compares to cleaning up the table after dinner and putting the dishes back in the cupboard. Take the following steps to close your aura after self healing or for closing your patient's aura after a healing session.

- Place one hand above the crown
- With your other hand, draw an orbit around the whole body
- Imagine a cocoon of pure positive energy surrounding them
- Mentally and physically separate yourself from the healing; step back one metre (three feet) to give your patient their own space
- Mentally and physically "cut" the connection between you and your patient with a downward chopping motion of your arms
- Thank Reiki for performing the healing with a blessing; gratitude is an important aspect of the healing process
- Confirm that both you and your patient are well grounded

    I would like to share one colourful experience concerning the closing of the aura. When I first met ten year old Kantu at "Mosoq Runa" children's home in Urubamba, Perú, she was withdrawn from everybody and expressed deep fear in her eyes. Throughout her first Reiki session, she held her eyes wide open, almost in alarm. This made sense, as I later found out that she had been abandoned as a baby. When we met two weeks later, she was smiling and much more trusting. She sighed deeply throughout the second session and continuously cleared her throat. Her relief was very evident. When she awoke, she reported in Spanish that she had lovely dreams of riding stars with all her friends. When we met for her third session, I received the warmest welcome. She ran up to me in the kitchen, gave me a big hug and asked if she could receive Reiki that day. She absorbed a great deal of energy and slumbered into a deep sleep.

    As I completed the healing, I intuitively felt that I should provide extra protection for her. As I closed her aura, I walked around seven times, visualising all the colours of the chakras: red, orange, yellow, green, blue, indigo and violet. I felt confident this would give her vital protection. When she awoke with a joyful look in her eyes, she reported that she had seen "arco iris," Spanish for rainbow. This was a beautiful example of communication through energy.

## Grounding

Many people feel a little bit spacey after receiving Reiki. Some people report feeling very light, so we joke that this is a great way to lose weight! An interesting story about grounding happened to one of my Thai students. Every night, San diligently performed a self-healing beginning at her brow chakra and then moving down her body. Invariably, she fell asleep during the process and never completed the full treatment. Consequently, the energy in her upper chakras was always very high and she was feeling spacey and out of touch. I suggested that she begin self-healings at her feet, then work upwards to her head, or until she fell asleep, whichever came first. At our next session, she reported that self-healing beginning from the feet was more effective and kept her well grounded.

To ground a person, place your hands on their feet. This helps them feel well connected to earth and completes the energy circuit. It prevents people from feeling spacey after a healing.

To cleanse yourself after a healing, hold your hands above your head and visualise a beam of white light showering down on your crown chakra. Allow the light of this "Reiki Shower" to rinse away any negative energy. Sweep your hands through your aura as described above. Additionally, imagine roots growing from your feet into the earth in order to ground yourself more thoroughly.

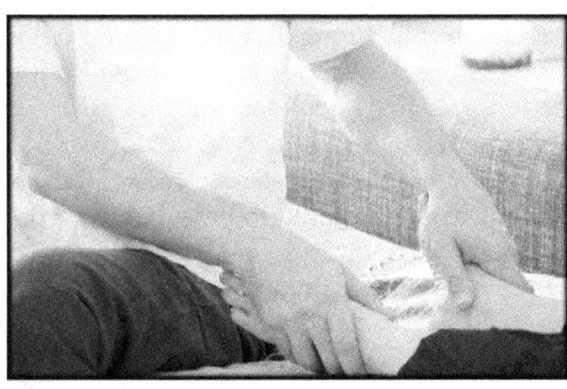

## Reflecting on a Healing Session

Some patients lie very still after receiving Reiki. I honour their peaceful posture and allow them to relax for a while. That gives me time to wash my hands, have a few glasses of water and freshen up. Eventually, you need to rouse your patient, have them sit up and reflect on the healing session. Serve them a glass of water, as Reiki may make them thirsty.

    Discuss the healing experience with your patient, asking what they experienced and felt. Then, share your own observations and feelings. Exchanging observations in this way puts the healing process in a holistic perspective, helping both people to participate in the co-healing nature of Reiki.

    Discuss the detoxification process that may follow a healing. This can include sleepiness, frequent urination, flatulence, diarrhoea, rashes, fever, excessive menstrual bleeding or temporary headaches. These symptoms are part of what is called a healing crisis. A healing crisis can take place when the body has been stimulated towards balance or purity. The body naturally aims towards health by releasing accumulated toxins through all channels of elimination. Keep in mind, all healing depends completely on what a person is ready to release. So, some people may cry after returning home while others may be very sleepy for a couple of days.

## After completing your Reiki Training Course

Most of our students come to study Reiki once a week for four or five weeks. This gives them time between classes to practise healing and fully attune their minds, bodies and souls to the energy. Unfortunately, many people believe they can complete a Reiki 1 class in just one day or one weekend.

    Some teachers proffer certificates immediately upon completion of the training. In my school, I establish the following requirements. These are intended to encourage students to practise consistently and diligently, rather than just grabbing their certificates and considering themselves trained.

1. Purify your home and healing area with Reiki, candles and incense
2. Perform a self healing every day for the first 21 days (at least) after receiving your attunement
3. Perform hands-on healings with at least 6 different people
4. Practise using Reiki with animals, plants and food
5. Receive distance healing from your teacher
6. Attend Reiki shares with your teacher and other students

I suggest maintaining contact with your teacher and other students whenever possible. It's nice to exchange ideas with people who understand you and Reiki. This inspires all students to persevere in their self-development and assure that they feel comfortable in a Reiki community, rather than feeling like a lonely outcast who has no one with whom to share their personal or mystical experiences.

Please don't rush immediately into Reiki 2. Take your time with Reiki 1. Develop your discipline, confidence and familiarity with all of the techniques suggested here. Gain enough experience that you know for certain you're ready to proceed to the next level. Some people feel ready in a few months, while others wait a year or two until they feel ready to approach the challenge of Reiki 2.

One client told me that she studied Reiki 1 and 2 in a single weekend but never received instruction in distance healing, purification and emotional changes that occur through the training programme. This was a strong testimonial against "instant healer" courses that you might see advertised. Please, take your time when you study and be sure you and your teacher very thoroughly cover every aspect of Reiki and the healing process.

---

**Authentic Certification**

The only authentic certification in any discipline is when you truly integrate the lessons and practices in your life and successfully overcome the barriers that limit you. At that stage, printed certification is totally redundant.

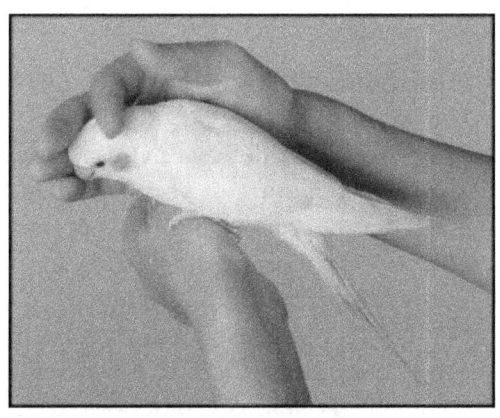

## Reiki for Animals

"Can I give Reiki to my dog? My gerbil?" Many of us are very close to our pets and want to share our energy with them. You can offer healings to cats, dogs, gerbils or any other animal. I don't wish to outline specific procedures, but I suggest that you adapt the techniques that you use with people as appropriate with your pet. Be sure to ask your pet if they want this healing (Yes! We all talk to our pets anyway, so this is no exception.). Offer your hands to them but be sure they have freedom to get up and move away when they've had enough. Some pets absolutely love Reiki while others show no interest at all. I remember when Yvette first learned Reiki. She went home and gave healings to her gerbil. One day, her hands became quite hot and her gerbil bit her! We interpreted this to mean that he was full and the healing was therefore complete. For a thorough description of using Reiki with animals, refer to "Animal Reiki" by Elizabeth Fulton and Kathleen Prasad.

Providing Reiki to animals supports the notion of Ahimsa. Dr. Gabriel Cousens writes that, "Ahimsa is an active stance in the world with a dynamic compassion for all of life. It is more than just non-violence ... Ahimsa means acting from a compassionate awareness and empathic identification that comes from reverence for life in every aspect of your day. It involves a personal responsibility to respect and work for the well being of all beings." You can understand why I emphasise Ahimsa because it closely parallels our work as Reiki healers. Sharing compassionate Reiki by healing animals is a powerful way to show loving kindness to the animal kingdom.

## Additional Healing Techniques

After you become familiar with the basic hand positions in Reiki, you may introduce additional techniques to your practice. Please don't try all of these at once! Experiment with these techniques one at a time on yourself. Then begin using them with other people, learning how and when to apply them. Joining a Reiki share with your teacher and other students provides an opportunity to test these techniques and include them in your healing sessions. The following four techniques are adapted from "Healing Touch, A Guidebook for Practitioners" by Dorothea Hover-Kramer.

## Ultrasound

This technique is similar to "sensing energy" described earlier. Ultrasound requires practice and focus to be strong enough to use it effectively to heal. Ultrasound is suitable for deep penetration of fractured bones, tumours, internal bleeding, arthritis and other internal physical issues. Your visualisation ability is a powerful component of this technique. Hold your thumb, index and middle fingers together; imagining a beam of light emitting from the confluence of your three fingers.

Mentally direct the beam of Reiki to heal deeply within the wound or fracture. Place your other hand behind the injury to complete the circuit of energy. Apply ultrasound for 3 to 5 minutes, keeping the beam moving continuously. In the case of serious injuries, seek professional medical attention as quickly as possible.

## Swivelling

Stand up during the healing session and allow your hips to swivel clockwise. This creates a centrifugal motion that pulls heaviness or negativity away from the patient's aura, through your body and into the ground. When I first learned Reiki, this movement occurred to me naturally. It was only several years later that I found the technique described in a book, confirming my intuitive movement.

The spinning motion removes negative energies from the patient which are then grounded through the legs of the healer. Try this motion while giving Reiki to each chakra. Be sure to keep yourself well grounded while swivelling, making sure any negative energies are firmly directed from your feet into the earth. If you like, you can purchase a "hula hoop" if you really want to practise this technique!

## Magnetic Pain Drain

Place your left hand on the area that hurts while holding your right hand towards the ground, away from the body. For example, you can apply this technique if your patient reports a severe migraine. Firmly intend to draw negative, painful energy from your patient to travel from your left hand, across your shoulders and out your right arm into the ground. Shake your right hand three times to discharge the energy. Continue until you feel the painful energy has been removed. Next, reverse your hands, putting your right hand on the area being healed while raising your left hand towards the sky to draw in healing energy.

This technique requires visualisation skills. Visualise the pain being pulled away and then imagine filling the area with light and warmth. This healing procedure requires that you have firmly established your mindfulness during healing and have practised protection techniques to ensure that no negative energies attach to you. Your role as a healer is to help remove unwanted energies, not to absorb them yourself!

## Spinal Energy Flow

This technique is applicable for patients with back pain. Most of the techniques described in this book refer to healing positions with the patient lying down flat on their backs. To conduct spinal energy flow it may be more comfortable for them to lie face down on the healing surface. Place one hand on the base of your patient's neck and the other hand at the base of their spine. Visualise the energy flowing back and forth between your hands like a wave. Hold this position until the energy flows smoothly and evenly. Imagine the energy removing blockages or pain. Maintain this position for 5 to 10 minutes.

Alternatively, place your fingertips directly on one side of the spine while your thumb is on the other side (as if picking up the vertebrae). Let the energy flow from your finger tips. This technique is suitable when pain is reported at a very specific location on the back.

## Conclusion

This chapter has covered all the basic techniques needed to practise Reiki 1 to heal yourself, family and friends plus several additional techniques to employ as you gain more experience. Experience is your greatest teacher, so it is essential that you practise as much as possible. This helps you develop your skills while family and friends benefit from the energy they receive from you. The next chapter looks closely at the nature and characteristics of each of the chakras. This information will further enhance your knowledge and awareness during healing situations.

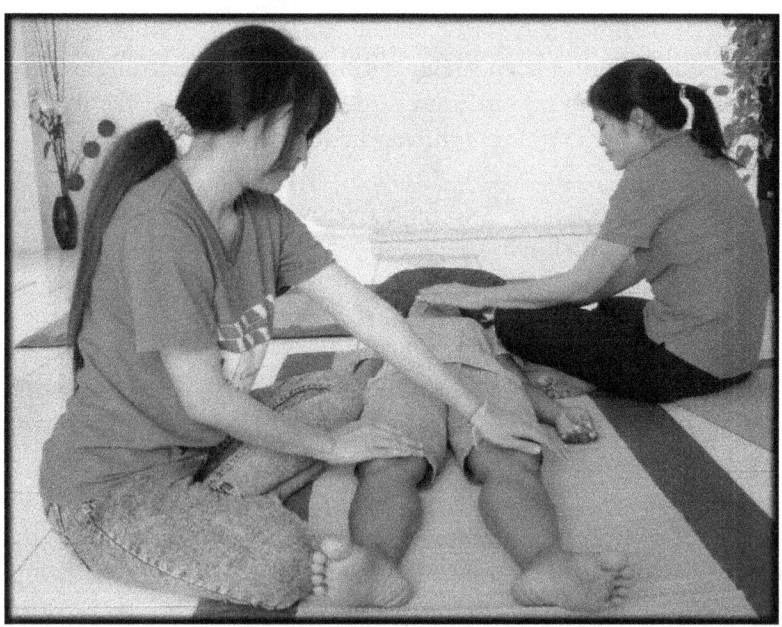

# Chapter Four

# Knowledge and Experience of Chakras

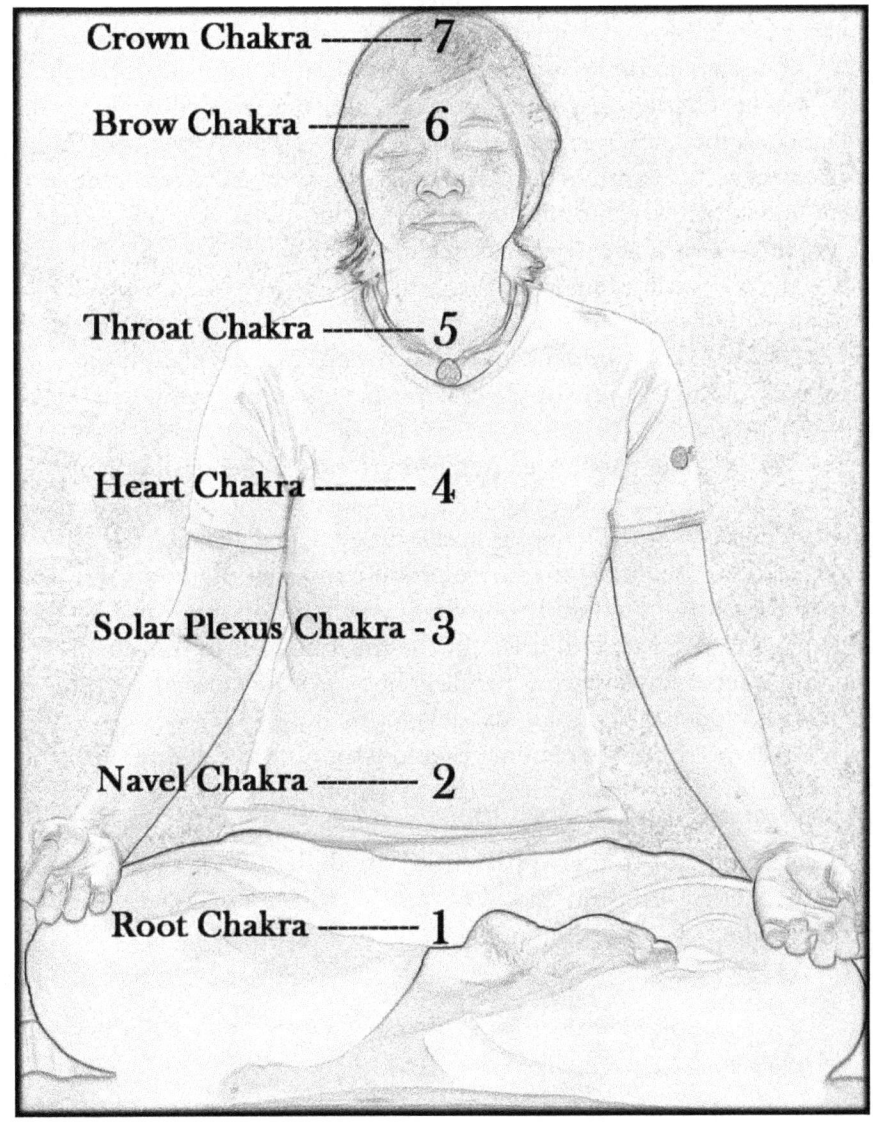

A chakra is an energy vortex located on the energetic body that corresponds to the physical body. A chakra is like a spinning disc of energy. Each of the seven major chakras on your body relates to specific spiritual, emotional and physical energies. Knowledge of chakras can help you with your healing practice by understanding your own characteristics and your patient's pattern of development.

This chapter discusses the characteristics of each chakra in its balanced, unbalanced, excessive and deficient states. During healings, it's helpful to be aware of the primary developmental issues that take place in each chakra. Combined with your intuition, you can interpret your patient's primary needs for healing.

Now, just because the picture shows where the chakras are located, is that sufficient for you to believe in something you have never seen? If you want to prove it to yourself, deep meditation will heighten your awareness of chakras far beyond what can be explained in these pages.

Some scientists have attempted to prove the existence of chakras through technology, but I'm not sure if you would believe this evidence or not. The most powerful evidence available that I know of is meditation. Join a meditation course sitting in noble silence for several days and your chakras will become as obvious to you as your eyes, ears and nose. In the meantime, read this chapter and you'll see many amazing parallels between the chakras and the Western model of psychological development.

Many of the characteristics and issues in this chapter are derived from "Eastern Body, Western Mind" by Anodea Judith. She provides a comprehensive analysis of the relationship between chakras and major trends in psychology including Freud, Piaget and Maslow. I highly recommend her book for future reading as you progress along your healing path.

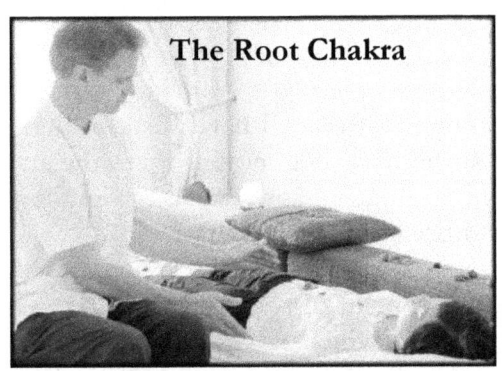

## The Root Chakra

Your root chakra begins to develop while you are still in the womb. It connects you to your family and environment. The primary issues of this chakra include self-preservation, getting enough to eat and feeling safe. The root chakra is concerned with physical identity, relates to the earth element and provides proper grounding. When healing others, place your hands on their hipbones or a respectful distance away from the genital area. The primary characteristics and issues related to the root chakra are listed below.

### Root Chakra Characteristics

| | |
|---|---|
| Location | Base of spine (perineum) |
| Healing Colour | Red |
| Element | Earth |
| Age of Development | 2nd trimester up to 12 months |
| Personal Rights | To be here and to have |
| Related Physical Organs | Bowels, large intestine, legs, feet |
| Balanced Characteristics | Stability, sense of trust, safety and security |
| Symptoms of Deficiency | Fearful, anxious, restless, poor discipline |
| Symptoms of Excess | Obesity, fear of change, addiction to security, material fixation |
| Emotional Traumas | Abandonment, neglect, family issues |
| Healing Practices | Yoga, grounding, review childhood experience |
| Positive Affirmation | The earth supports me and fulfils my needs |

For the last couple of years, I have been starting the majority of healing sessions at the feet, then moving up to the knees and then the root chakra. This approach assures a solid grounding and a firm foundation for the entire healing experience.

During a healing with Anthony, I was giving Reiki to his root chakra. Intuitively, the thought of beef popped into my mind. I asked him how often he ate beef, which was quite frequently. With further inquiry, he explained his digestive and elimination troubles. Combining knowledge of the chakra system with my intuitive awareness of a "beef issue," I suggested that he gradually decrease his consumption of beef. A few weeks later, he reported greatly improved digestion and elimination, feeling much better with less beef in his system. This allowed his body to work more efficiently and release accumulated toxins from his digestive system. Reiki, in conjunction with intuition and life style change, helped him improve his own health.

Since this chakra is concerned with the bowels and elimination, it's not surprising when a patient reports diarrhoea after a thorough healing of the root chakra. Diarrhoea is the body's internal cleansing system working to eliminate both physical and emotional wastes that have accumulated in the body. I remember one woman in Cusco, Perú who I gave Reiki to one evening just before she was going to a pub. Later, she blamed me for causing diarrhoea and she couldn't party that night. Maybe we should have been more selective with the timing of her healing session.

## Navel (Sacral) Chakra

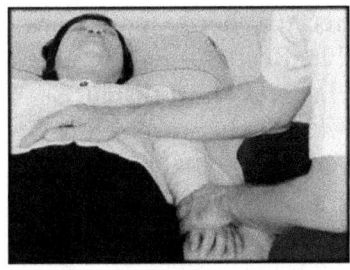

Your navel chakra is the second chakra to develop when you are still an infant. It's located two centimetres (one inch) below your navel. You might call it the pleasure or sensual chakra because it relates to exploration through sensory experience and self-gratification. The principal identity of this chakra is emotional, as indicated by the symptoms of excess or deficiency in the chart below. Notice the correspondence between the physical and emotional issues in the characteristics of this chakra. Physical abuse leads to emotional suffering, while emotional abuse leads to physical suffering. For example, this chakra is concerned with emotional sexual issues and physical sexual organs. Knowing the characteristics of the navel chakra, consider how positive affirmations can best be used to support you or your patient's healing process.

### Naval Chakra Characteristics

| | |
|---|---|
| Location | Lower abdomen, 2 centimetres (1 inch) below the navel |
| Healing Colour | Orange |
| Element | Water |
| Age of Development | 6 months to 2 years |
| Personal Rights | To feel and to have pleasure |
| Related Physical Organs | Reproductive organs, urinary system, kidneys, bladder, lower back |
| Balanced Characteristics | Graceful, good EQ, ability to experience pleasure |
| Symptoms of Deficiency | Rigid body and attitudes, poor social skills, denial of pleasure |
| Symptoms of Excess | Excessive emotions, emotional dependency |
| Emotional Traumas | Neglect, rejection, sexual abuse, denial of feelings |
| Healing Practices | Movement therapy, practise healthy pleasures |
| Positive Affirmation | I deserve pleasure in my life. |

At one of our first Reiki courses at Wongsanit Ashram in Thailand, we had a real scare concerning the second chakra. Students were exchanging energy when Wanla reported that her kidneys were feeling very hot and becoming uncomfortable. Recognising this as a deep cleansing, we continued, but kept our hands a short distance away to moderate the energy flow. The day after the course completed, we received a worried phone call that she had blood in her urine. At first we were scared, but then realised that Reiki was working to remove impurities and blockages from her urinary system. The symptoms passed the next day and she felt better. Three years have passed and she has felt fine ever since. All the symptoms completely cleared. This story is an important reminder that we need to know our patient's condition before a healing and make them aware of potential detoxification processes that may occur following a healing. Detoxification at this chakra can involve the urinary and reproductive systems. Other students have reported excessive menstrual flow shortly after studying Reiki. This also indicates the body's natural efforts to cleanse itself thoroughly.

## Solar Plexus Chakra

By the age of two, your solar plexus chakra is opening and gaining energy. This accounts for the phenomenon that parents refer to as the "terrible twos." If children are supported in their growth at this stage, it leads to healthy development of self-esteem and empowers children to mature. Notice the symbolic correlation between the "fire" element and the right to take "action." If a child is hampered at this stage of development, it may contribute to life long lack of self-confidence and fear of taking action. On the other hand, if a child is overly spoiled during this time, the solar plexus may respond with aggressive or stubborn behaviour, indicating excessive ego.

Another possibility is that children with aggression or stubbornness are compensating for weaknesses in their first or second chakras. I call the solar plexus the "action chakra" because healing it helps people take necessary and appropriate action to get their lives on track. This can include taking action in terms of changing jobs, moving house or pursuing a dream.

### Solar Plexus Chakra Characteristics

| | |
|---|---|
| Location | Solar plexus, mid abdomen |
| Healing Colour | Yellow |
| Element | Fire |
| Age of Development | 18 months to 4 years |
| Personal Rights | To act and to be an individual (self-definition) |
| Related Physical Organs | Digestive system, stomach, pancreas, gall bladder, liver |
| Balanced Characteristics | Responsible, reliable, effective will, confident |
| Symptoms of Deficiency | Low energy, weak will, low self-esteem |
| Symptoms of Excess | Aggressive, controlling, stubborn, hyperactive |
| Emotional Traumas | Shaming, authoritarianism, domination of will, abuse |
| Healing Practices | Stress control, vigorous exercise |
| Positive Affirmation | I have the right to take action. |

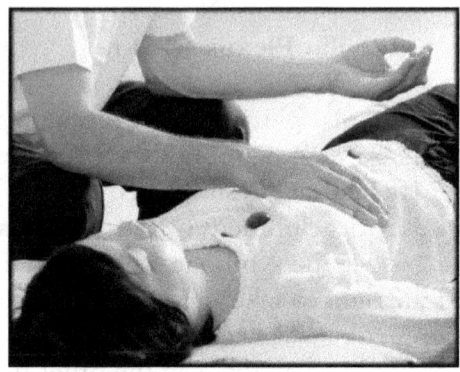

The following correspondence demonstrates several issues that inhabit the solar plexus, including aggression, responsibility and self-definition:

Hi Tom,

I finally got to the bottom of the issue that came to the surface during our last Reiki session. If you recall, you sensed that the age of 6 was the time of the problem and that it was about responsibility and loss of childhood. I couldn't quite relate to this as I had been focusing on my parents and nothing quite resonated.

This morning, it suddenly came to me that the issue is with my sister. A whole lot of hatred for her came whooshing out. She was constantly a "drama queen," manipulating everyone with tears and tantrums. When I was 6, she would have been 4 or 5 years old. I remember that we continually had to appease her to keep the peace and Mum relied on me to let my wishes go unheeded if they clashed with my sister's.

My mother put me in charge of her. I had to take her to Sunday School and it involved crossing a busy road. I recalled that I felt very frightened of crossing the road with no pedestrian lights to help. There was a feeling of heaviness, of too much responsibility beyond my capabilities.

What about me? Now I understand what I felt about my sister at that age but what I hadn't, until now, been able to admit to myself, since it clashed with my ego-identification as the dependable, reliable, responsible child. As I relived the stressful scene, the Reiki energy helped it to shift and clear and I felt much better afterwards. I wonder if any more 6 year old painful memories are still lurking! I'll keep digging.

Best regards,

Anne

A little later, Anne wrote,

> I gave myself Reiki daily over the following week and more of the fear of being overburdened with responsibility as a child came to the surface and was healed. Reiki has been a valuable tool to help me clear away painful and fearful emotions from my body, both when someone else gives me healing or when I send it to myself.

Her letters reveal the issues that she is now releasing more than 40 years after the fact. The description of her younger sister's behaviour indicates excessive energy in the solar plexus. Reiki empowered and encouraged Anne to return to her childhood memories to re-evaluate and release old feelings and outdated patterns of behaviour. The healing process is helping her recognise her own highly demanding sense of responsibility. She is now establishing a more effective concept of responsibility in her adult life, which is bringing her great relief.

# Heart Chakra

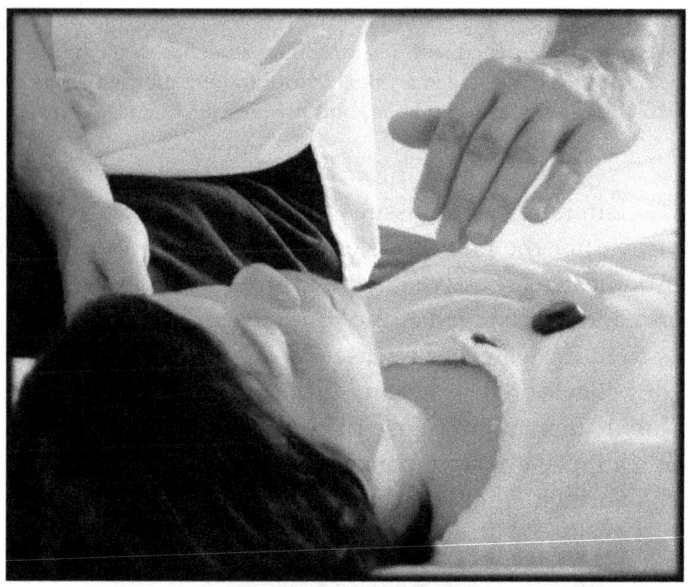

You might call this the "social chakra" because it is primarily concerned with human relationships. Through this chakra, we give and receive love. In modern society, the concept of love tends to be reduced to romantic love with relatively less emphasis on awareness of family, fraternal, community and universal love that surround and support us throughout our lives. The pictures show comfortable and appropriate hand positions for healing the fourth chakra. Maintain a respectful distance when healing women. I usually place a rose quartz on the heart chakra throughout the duration of a healing session to nurture universal love. See the section concerning crystals in chapter six for more details.

   Look through this chart to see which characteristics resonate with you. If for example you are very demanding and clinging, this indicates an excess of energy in your heart chakra. You may need to "share" the excess energy with your weaker chakras. See the section concerning connecting chakras at the end of this chapter for further explanation about sharing energies between chakras.

## Heart Chakra Characteristics

| | |
|---:|:---:|
| Location | Chest, heart |
| Healing Colour | Green (and pink) |
| Element | Air |
| Age of Development | 4 to 7 years |
| Personal Rights | To love and be loved |
| Related Physical Organs | Heart, lungs, thymus, breasts, arms |
| Balanced Characteristics | Compassionate, loving, empathetic, peaceful, good immunity |
| Symptoms of Deficiency | Anti-social, withdrawn, cold, judgmental, intolerant, depression |
| Symptoms of Excess | Demanding, clinging, jealousy |
| Emotional Traumas | Abandonment, loss, criticism, conditional love, betrayal |
| Healing Practices | Breathing exercises (Pranayama), journaling, forgiveness practice |
| Positive Affirmation | I am lovable and loving. |

In my own experience, my intense life-time stress gradually decreased after studying Reiki 2. After completing the course, I allowed myself to take a few days off of work, which was very uncharacteristic of me. I also started scaling back the amount of work that I assigned my students at university, much to their relief, and softened my expectations of myself. One afternoon, I gave myself Reiki and found myself crying and shaking, eventually slipping into depression. After a little sleep, I awoke with awareness that I had a right to be happy and a right to be

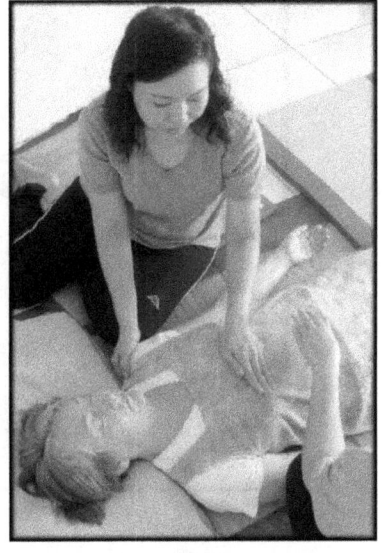

loved. These were very important realisations for me. I perceived that I no longer had to work so hard in a futile effort to get people to love me more. I finally realised that I could be happy; I was warmly loved and didn't need to be perfect! These were very empowering insights for me. Ultimately, the concept of personal rights made sense at the deepest level of my being. Prior to that, somewhere in my heart I believed that I had no right to be happy and I was never good enough to deserve love. All of these insights related to self-acceptance, the basic orientation of the heart chakra.

## Throat Chakra

I often call this the communication chakra because it's used for expressing ideas and communicating your true self as formulated in the heart. The throat chakra is oriented towards communication and creativity. Maybe we should call it the poetry chakra! Compare the balanced, deficient and excessive characteristics of this chakra and you will recognise how some of these patterns manifest in your family, friends and in your self.

As we mature, all of us experience life in unique ways. We respond to life experiences while life reciprocates with lessons that we need to learn and incorporate into our lives. During the age that the throat chakra develops, a child is actively expressing, or attempting to express, who they are, what they want, how they feel and what they think. At this stage, the "little human" seems increasingly complete, expressing the strengths and weaknesses of all five chakras that have developed up until this stage of life.

Interestingly, the human body seems "bottle necked" at the throat like a terrible traffic jam between the intensely emotional heart and the thought laden mind. The throat, relatively speaking, is much smaller than the heart and mind, so it often suffers from blockage. This is particularly true in a culture that believes children should be seen and not heard. The throat chakra is often the most sensitive of all chakras, so it must be approached cautiously. Keep a slight distance away from a person's throat, as this is a sensitive area both physically and energetically. Refer to the accompanying photos for suitable healing positions.

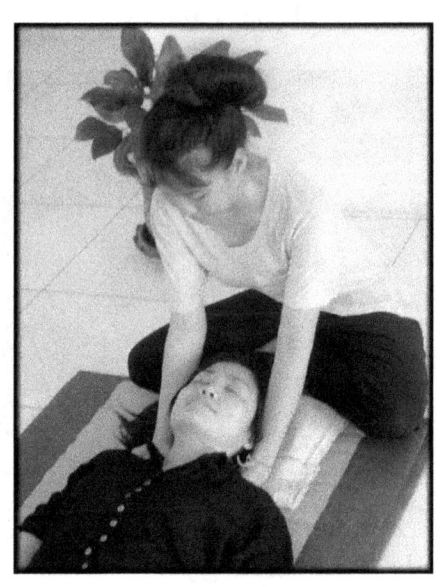

## Throat Chakra Characteristics

| | |
|---:|:---:|
| **Location** | Throat |
| **Healing Colour** | Sky blue |
| **Element** | Sound |
| **Age of Development** | 7 to 12 years |
| **Personal Rights** | To speak and be heard, creativity |
| **Related Physical Organs** | Throat, ears, voice box, neck, jaw |
| **Balanced Characteristics** | Good listener, clear communication, creative |
| **Symptoms of Deficiency** | Fear of speaking, weak voice, introversion |
| **Symptoms of Excess** | Too talkative, gossiping, poor listening, interrupting |
| **Emotional Traumas** | Lies, verbal abuse, authoritarian parents, criticism |
| **Healing Practices** | Loosen neck and shoulders, singing, journaling |
| **Positive Affirmation** | I have a right to my creativity. |

As an example of the sensitivity of this chakra, I was sending distance healing to a colleague with thyroid problems. I sensed fire furiously shooting forth from her throat. I had to maintain a psychic distance of more than a metre (three feet) in order to conduct the healing. In another example, I remember sensing intense fear at an Australian man's throat chakra. We discussed how he could transform his fear into courage. Intuitively, a suggestion came to me that he should practise the lion Yoga pose. This resonated with him strongly as he recognised how he had been broken down by the circumstances of his life that made him fearful and withdrawn.

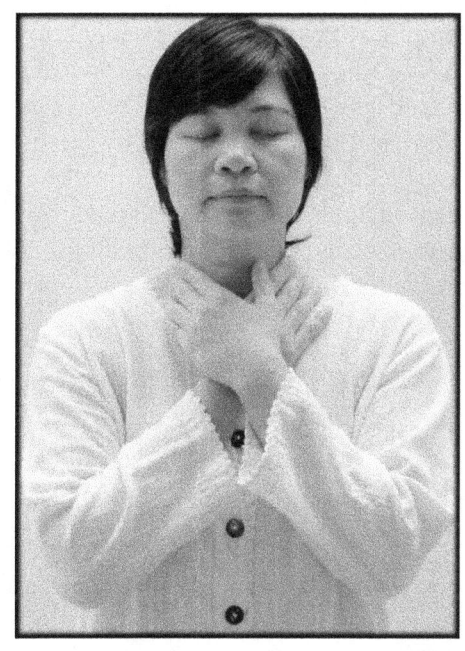

On that note, I suggest seeking further information on how to apply Yoga as part of your personal healing programme. "Raja Yoga" by Swami Kriyananda provides detailed explanations of how Yoga works therapeutically to heal all levels of being. You will find that Reiki and Yoga complement each other very effectively. Several exercises for the throat chakra are explained in chapter seven.

The throat chakra is infinitely complex and manifests a wide variety of issues that you may observe in your day to day life. A Thai woman, Sandra, first came to our Reiki clinic seeking relief from long term low energy, mild depression and always feeling tired. I felt her tension and I sensed isolation at her brow. My intuition suggested an image of a broken plate while healing her solar plexus. We discussed this image and realised that it symbolised her broken will. This gave good insight into the nature of her trouble and the path towards healing.

During the session, Sandra felt as if she had left the room for quite a while and eventually returned feeling better, with tears streaming from her eyes as she stared blankly at the ceiling. On her third healing, we had a strong breakthrough. We discussed her "not knowing" what she wants. At her throat chakra, she experienced an epiphany that she didn't really know how to want, how to expect or how to hope. She seemed constrained by unspoken expectations of her. Over the next several weeks of healings, her energy increased, depression subsided and she opened up sufficiently to join a Reiki 1 class. Since then, she has been one of our most enthusiastic partners at Reiki shares. She has also become much more active professionally and socially, opening up in all aspects of her life. In her own words, she writes,

> Reiki saved my life. I came to Reiki when I was at the very lowest point in my life. I was exhausted, depressed and not able to think of anything or get anything done. The healing provided me the necessary strength to recover. With Reiki I learned to let go all of too many things I had been keeping. I also recognised my fear, how to live with it and how to be free from it. Practicing Reiki I can feel more energy, peace and hope. Reiki is my lifeline.

> Thank you very much,

> Sandra

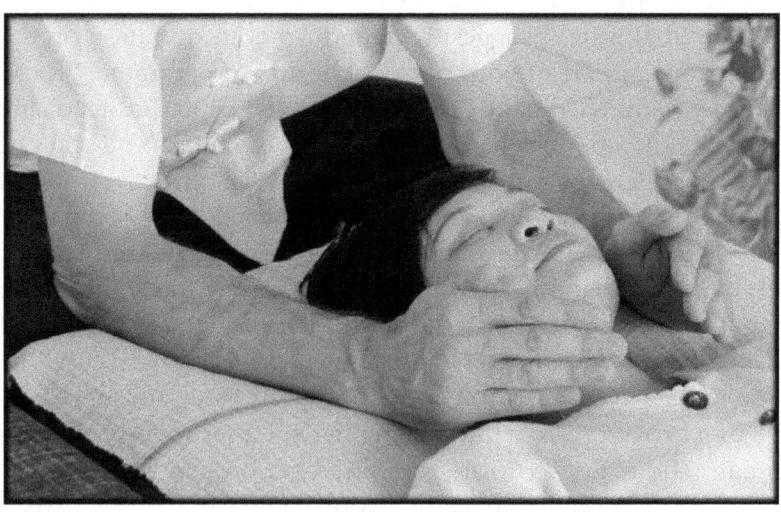

## Brow Chakra

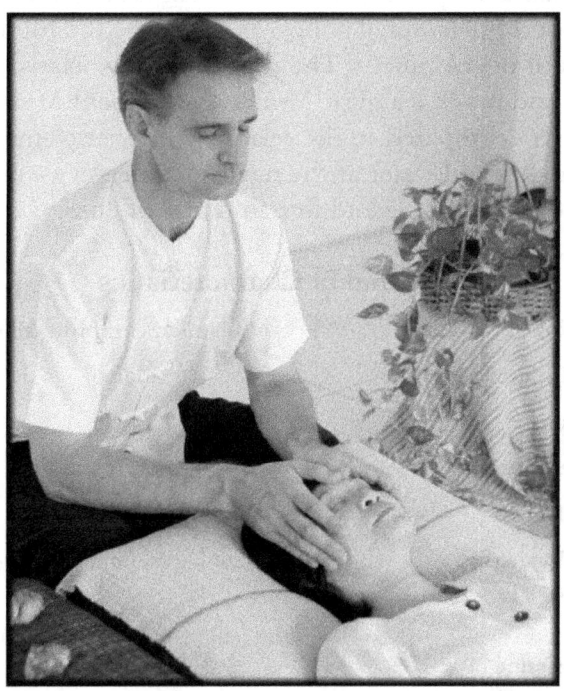

When I first learned Reiki, I began healing sessions at the brow chakra because most people have very active brains leading to stress, headaches and tension. Over the years, I have shifted my starting position to the feet, gradually working towards the higher energy centres in the head. Why? By the time I've healed the lower five chakras, a person is very well grounded, relaxed and receptive; they are better prepared for receiving energy in the highly active brain.

At the brow chakra, begin with your hands 25 centimetres (12 inches) from your patient's forehead, gradually coming closer and making contact. One difficulty while giving Reiki to this chakra is that it seems funny talking with your patient from an upside down position. Therefore, discuss the nature of the healing beforehand. In some healings, conversation is the essential element of the healing process. In other cases, it's appropriate to lead a personalised, guided meditation that involves visualisation.

A quick look at the information in the chart below reveals that this chakra is very much related to our capacity as healers. The brow chakra is concerned with intuition, imagination and symbolic thinking. Your personal interest in Reiki healing is one indication that your brow chakra is opening and you are embarking on a journey of light, far beyond the material concerns that were the foundation of earlier stages of development. The third eye is associated with clairvoyance and psychic ability. Notice the element of the brow chakra is "light" compared to the relatively heavier elements of earth at the root chakra and water at the navel chakra. As we develop, we become increasingly subtle and fine in terms of energy.

## Brow Chakra Characteristics

| | |
|---|---|
| Location | Forehead, middle of brow (third eye) |
| Healing Colour | Indigo |
| Element | Light |
| Age of Development | Adolescence |
| Personal Rights | To see (self reflection) |
| Related Physical Organs | Brain, eyes, pituitary gland |
| Balanced Characteristics | Intuitive, imaginative, good memory, symbolic thinking |
| Symptoms of Deficiency | Insensitive, poor vision, poor memory, lack of imagination |
| Symptoms of Excess | Delusions, obsessions, difficulty concentrating, nightmares |
| Emotional Traumas | Violent environment, shame, refusal to see truth |
| Healing Practices | Meditation, create visual art, guided visualisation |
| Positive Affirmation | I see all things clearly. |

In "Plants as Teachers," Matthew Wood writes that "spiritual vision is an extension of imagination. Healing is an art that uses the imagination." This becomes important if you want to use guided visualisation in your Reiki healing practice. While at first using Reiki on family and friends, you may prefer to maintain silent during healings. As you progress, gain more confidence and your intuition becomes more finely tuned, guided visualisations may become an essential aspect of your healing practice.

I once led a guided meditation for Daniel, a friend from Lima who held very negative childhood memories. Using Reiki along with guided visualisation helped him recall more positive memories of walking along the ocean holding his parents' hands. This was an effective image for him to replace the previously dominant memory of having an abusive father. In one sense, we "went back in time." In another sense, we performed "memory replacement therapy" which is a lot less risky than the chemical procedure "hormone replacement therapy."

Be careful when using visualisation with your patients. Be sure to respect their privacy, always asking permission to proceed along this path. I don't mean that your patient will be hypnotised and you can manipulate their memories, but be aware how deeply your patient trusts you with their well being and their deepest secrets or memories. The deeper you go into a healing, the greater your responsibility to respect and honour the sanctity of their life.

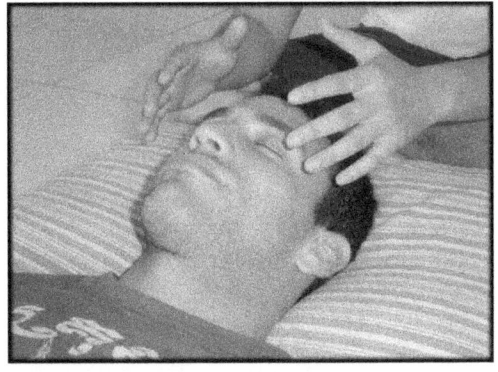

In reviewing the healing stories for this book, I realise how much I learned about Reiki while travelling across South America as a Reiki Master a few years ago. One morning, we were all sitting over breakfast in Sucre, Bolivia and got on the subject of Reiki. One woman was a registered psychologist from Britain who insisted that she could never use Reiki with her patients because it would be illegal to touch them. While it's essential to exercise propriety in any healing situation, it seems that her legal argument somewhat undermined the notion that trust needs to be firmly established to facilitate an effective co-healing experience. On the other hand, Emma, an Australian volunteer working in Bolivia was very interested in experiencing Reiki so we scheduled a healing for later that afternoon.

I closed my eyes and requested Reiki to perform the healing. My hands gently approached her brow chakra and the word "funeral" instantly flashed in my mind. Trusting the importance of this image, I asked her if somebody close to her had recently died. She began crying, relating the story of a close friend who had committed suicide.

Her sadness was clearly palpable in her aura. Normally, messages do not come with such obvious signs. Most intuitive messages are more subtle, just a feeling or a hunch about what may be troubling a patient. We discussed the implications of her friend's death and how heavily it was weighing down her heart. I asked her if she wanted to release the pain and obligations that persisted in her mind. She hesitated for a moment before saying "no," she wanted and needed to hold on to the situation for a little longer. Very importantly, this was her personal right to hold onto her pain. I honoured and respected her decision. I was confident that when she was ready, she would make her own decisions regarding her troubling situation.

## Crown Chakra

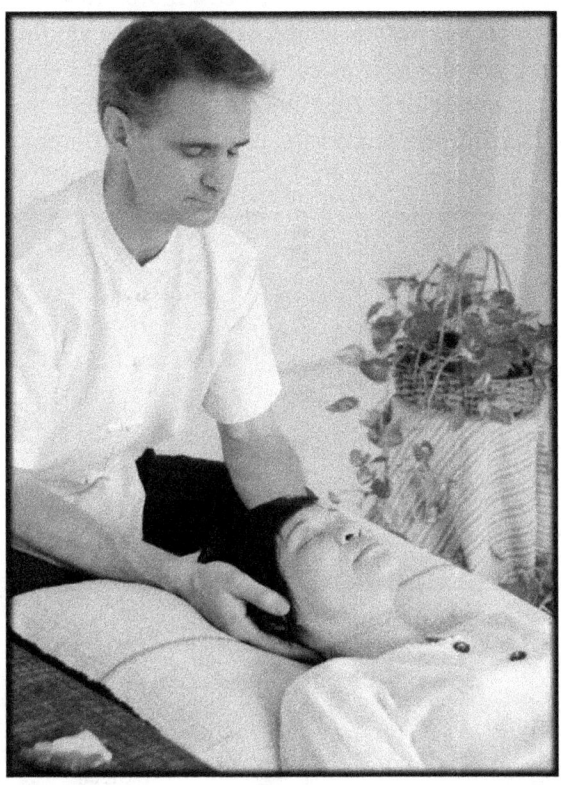

The crown chakra is the divine chakra, connecting us to universal energy and sacred peace. It's no wonder that in many Asian cultures, it's inappropriate to touch the top of the head, especially on an older person. Keep this in mind when providing healings. It might be more appropriate to cradle the head from behind as shown in the photo above, rather than directly touching the crown, to respect a person's divine centre.

The identity of this chakra is universal. Meditation aims to transcend the small individual ego in deference to a universal self. Operating from this level of being, our orientation reaches towards wisdom and transcendence. "Self" takes on a very different meaning than it did when we were children and our solar plexus was just beginning to blossom. The crown chakra tunes us in to "universal self." The concepts of universal self and universal meditation are explored thoroughly in chapter nine.

Common ailments related to the crown chakra include migraines, amnesia and coma. Deficiency in the crown chakra may indicate excessive energy in the lower chakras manifesting as materialism or greed. Balancing the chakras as explained in chapter three is one way to address excessive or deficient chakras. A more complex technique known as connecting the chakras is explained at the end of this chapter.

### Crown Chakra Characteristics

| | |
|---|---|
| Location | Cerebral cortex, top of skull |
| Healing Colour | Violet |
| Element | Wisdom |
| Age of Development | Early adulthood onwards |
| Personal Rights | To know and to learn |
| Related Physical Organs | Brain, pineal gland |
| Balanced Characteristics | Analytical, intelligent, thoughtful, open minded, wise |
| Symptoms of Deficiency | Spiritual cynicism, rigid beliefs, materialism |
| Symptoms of Excess | Intellectualisation, spiritual addiction, confusion |
| Emotional Traumas | Forced religiosity, blind obedience |
| Healing Practices | Meditation, examine belief system |
| Positive Affirmation | I am guided by inner wisdom. |

Another perspective concerning spiritual development is explained very explicitly by Chogyam Trungpa. He says,

> The ego is able to convert everything to its own use, even spirituality. We need to step out of ego's constant desire for a higher, more spiritual, more transcendental version of knowledge, religion or whatever the ego is seeking. The impulse of searching for something is, in itself, a hang-up.

These words of caution are very helpful if you fall into the trap of spiritual addiction. As a perfectionist, I recognise that I must pay heed to this issue, being careful not to push Reiki and to avoid trying to persuade people who don't believe in it. My personal development also requires that I don't push myself too hard to be spiritual. I need to keep my ego in check moment by moment.

You've probably met people who don't believe in any religion, meditation or healing energy. Spiritual cynicism is not necessarily bad; it just shows a deficiency of energy at the crown chakra. A cynic is most likely not to believe in Reiki and will probably not be calling you any time soon to request a healing. This is a good example of when we must be careful not to push Reiki on anybody. As discussed earlier, we need to respect people as they are and for what they believe. There's not much point in trying to persuade somebody to believe in Reiki or to experience it because they simply are not at that stage of their lives where such things are important to them. It would be like persuading a teenager who loved rap music to listen to one of Verdi's operas. Let people believe what they believe and leave it at that.

If the subject does arise in conversation with a person with very strong doubts about Reiki, it may be wise to explain it in terms of quantum physics, rather than in terms of chakras. This will keep the conversation concrete and technical rather than mystical. Also bear in mind that you are under no obligation to explain Reiki to anybody. Simply saying, "it's sort of like meditating" may be enough to gently bring closure to the topic when necessary.

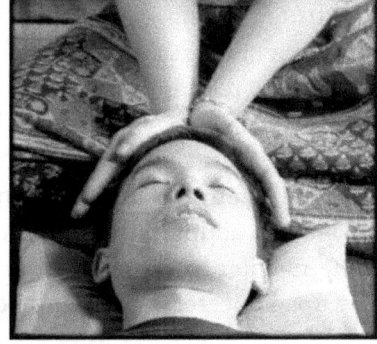

## Acupressure

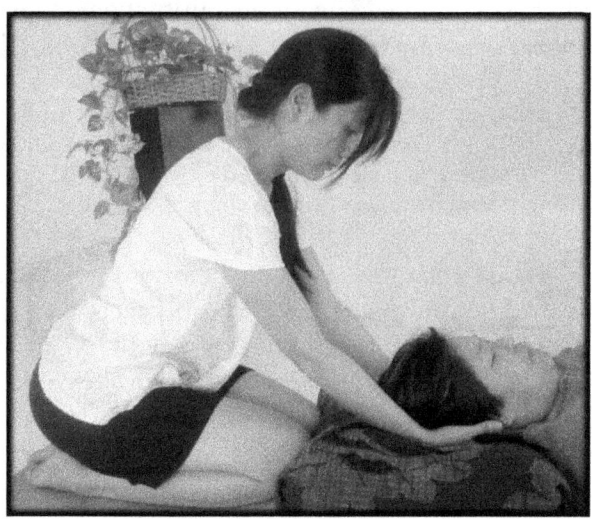

While receiving Reiki at her crown chakra, I remember Pam saying, "It feels like somebody is massaging my brain!" Actually, there is a massage technique you can use while healing the crown chakra called "stillpoint spinal alignment."

With your hands cradling your patient's skull as shown in the photo above, gently massage the upper neck where it meets the skull. Probe with your fingertips, feeling for the stillpoints, the soft indentations where the skull meets the neck. Press and hold these points for a few minutes to increase the flow of energy in the spine. Technically, the stillpoints are identified as the bladder-10 acupuncture points in Chinese Traditional Medicine. Pressure or gentle massage on these points releases tension and helps relieve migraines. You may feel a tingling sensation in your fingertips or your patient may report a sharp, tingling feeling on their neck.

This technique balances the pulse of the spinal fluid. As you apply pressure, observe the rhythm of your patient's breathing. After several minutes, they may deeply sigh and their breathing will slow down. This acupressure technique can be very effective and is not invasive like acupuncture. Please, don't stick your grandmother's sewing needles into the acupuncture points! Just the touch of your fingertips is perfectly safe and adequate for releasing pressure.

# Guided Chakra Meditation

This meditation procedure is suitable for studying Reiki at any level. As you become more familiar with the chakra system, you can develop this procedure to suit your own style. Sit in the lotus position. Close your eyes and follow your breath as described in chapter two. This meditation is a powerful way to review your knowledge of chakras while sending energy to relevant issues. The following example concerns the root chakra. Focus on just one chakra for your entire meditation, which may last 20 to 30 minutes. Each day, proceed to meditate on the subsequent chakra. Refer to the sections above for specific information concerning each chakra. Speak to yourself gently yet firmly, maintaining strong mindfulness throughout the session. Your script, although spontaneous, may follow along these lines:

- Place your hands on your root chakra and ask Reiki to flow
- Remain silent between each sentence for the duration of 3 or 4 breaths
- Imagine red light healing your root
- The root chakra develops during the first year of life; please heal any issues from that time in my life
- The personal rights of this chakra are to be and to have; please strengthen my awareness and exercise of these rights
- Maintain awareness of your breathing
- The root relates to my sense of stability, sense of trust and grounding
- Physically, the root chakra deals with the bowels and large intestines; please heal these organs for me
- Emotionally, it relates to issues of abandonment, neglect and security; please heal these issues for me
- Symptoms of weakness include fear and anxiety; please support me to overcome these weaknesses
- Continue your meditation, breathing in and out, allowing Reiki to flow abundantly

# Positive Affirmation Meditation

Every chakra has its own rights and needs. First, be aware that you need to accept any weakness or deficiencies as a true part of your nature. This does not imply that you must live with those weaknesses your whole life. When you have effectively learned from those challenges and you make a conscious decision to release them, you are truly ready for healing and transformation. In the following meditation, focus on each chakra for 5 minutes to empower your healing process. A complete meditation on all 7 chakras requires about 35 minutes.

1. Make a positive affirmation for each chakra.
2. Inhale deeply and release tension with each exhale.
3. Place your hands over your root chakra, feel life force and your sense of belonging to the earth; confirm your sense of safety and security; affirm "The earth supports me and fulfils my needs." Let the Reiki flow.
4. Move your hands to your navel chakra; sense that your body is well balanced; affirm "I deserve pleasure in my life."
5. Put your hands on your solar plexus chakra, draw energy in from the universe to empower your action; affirm and feel "I have the right to take action." Visualise yourself taking action.
6. Rest your hands on your heart chakra and feel the flow of unconditional love towards others and feel their love flowing into you; affirm "I am lovable and loving." Visualise family and friends who love you; feel the love; really feel it.
7. Place your hands on your throat chakra; confirm your ability to express your being; affirm "I have a right to my creativity." Visualise yourself engaging in a new creative project.
8. Bring your hands to your brow chakra and ask Reiki to strengthen your intuition; affirm "I see all things clearly."
9. Reach to your crown chakra and feel your connection to the infinite; affirm "I am guided by inner wisdom."

# Connecting the Chakras

With Reiki 1, students focus on healing one chakra at a time. As you gain more sensitivity to energy, you can begin a more complex healing pattern. Determine which chakras need to be energised by scanning (see chapter three) or using a pendulum (see chapter six). Place one hand on the weak chakra and put your other hand on the chakra above it for 1 to 3 minutes. This shares energy from a stronger chakra to raise the energy of the weaker one. Keep one hand on the weak chakra while moving the other hand up one more chakra until the energy stabilises. Do this for each chakra above, all the way to the crown.

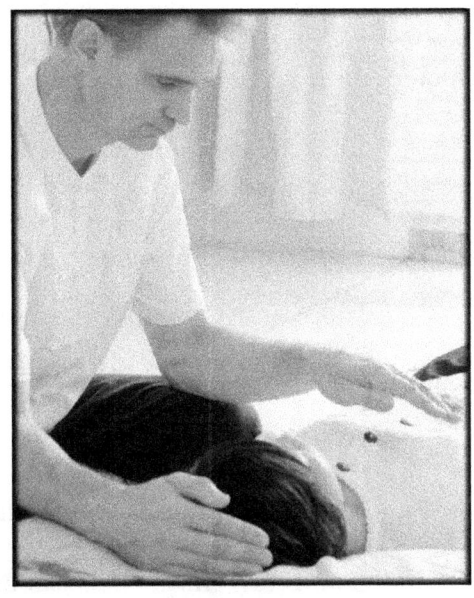

Proceed to connect the weak chakra to all of the chakras below it. Keep one hand on the weak chakra and place your other hand on each of the chakras below until all the chakras have been connected to the weak one. To summarise the procedure, review this example for connecting the heart chakra to the upper chakras.

1. Left hand on heart, right hand near throat
2. Left hand on heart, right hand on brow
3. Left hand on heart, right hand on crown

Now, connect the heart chakra with the lower chakras.

1. Right hand on heart, left hand on solar plexus
2. Right hand on heart, left hand on navel chakra
3. Right hand on heart, left hand near root chakra

This completes the connection of the heart to the other six chakras, absorbing energy from all of them. While connecting chakras, consider the following implications. For example, when connecting your patient's heart chakra to other chakras, questions such as these can guide your therapeutic communication:

What would you like to express (chakra 5)
concerning your emotions (chakra 4)?

How do you feel (chakra 4)
about your creative expression (chakra 5)?

How do you feel (chakra 4)
about your actions (chakra 3)?

What action can you take (chakra 3)
to address your feelings (chakra 4)?

Connecting the chakras can be a very powerful way to round out your character. After reviewing the characteristics of each of the chakras, you will have a better idea of your own strengths and weaknesses. If you find, for example, that your solar plexus is super-charged as evidenced by very high self-confidence and a highly driven personality, this suggests an excess of energy in your third chakra. If at the same time you discover that you have cysts or tumours in your reproductive system, this suggests a weak or closed second chakra. By analysing your personal traits and physical symptoms, determine which chakras are most in need of healing and connection.

## Chakra Spread

This technique is used for severe emotional or physical pain. It brings a person to a deeper level of healing than most other techniques. It should be reserved for special needs and sacred moments in healing. As always, practise this technique on yourself until you become familiar with the procedure. When you are ready, introduce it to your healing practice with others. Ask your patient to sit in a chair while you are standing in front of them. Begin by grounding yourself well; affirm that you are mentally stable and physically well connected to the earth.

1. Place your hands on your patient's feet for one or two minutes to be sure they are well grounded.

2. Hold your patient's hands in yours for one or two minutes to open their palm chakras.

3. Walk behind your patient and place both hands on their crown chakra.

4. Open their crown chakra by gently and slowly lifting both of your hands up and out as far as you can reach, like the wings of an eagle. Perform this movement three times.

5. If other chakras are in need of opening, spread them in the same manner.

6. Complete the healing process by closing their aura as described in chapter three.

## Conclusion

This chapter has presented many concepts concerning each of the chakras, but this does not mean that you must memorise and know every detail of every chakra during every healing. The most effective way to approach this information is to review it from time to time, but be sure not to over intellectualise during your healings.

The essence of Reiki is simply to place your hands on each chakra and let the energy flow. If concepts or images come to mind, this shows that your intuition is working to inform you how to proceed. If your mind is quiet and still, that's great! As my Reiki Master Danielle always reminds her students, "release all expectations during each healing. Just let the energy flow." When necessary, this technical information on each of the chakras is always available for further reference.

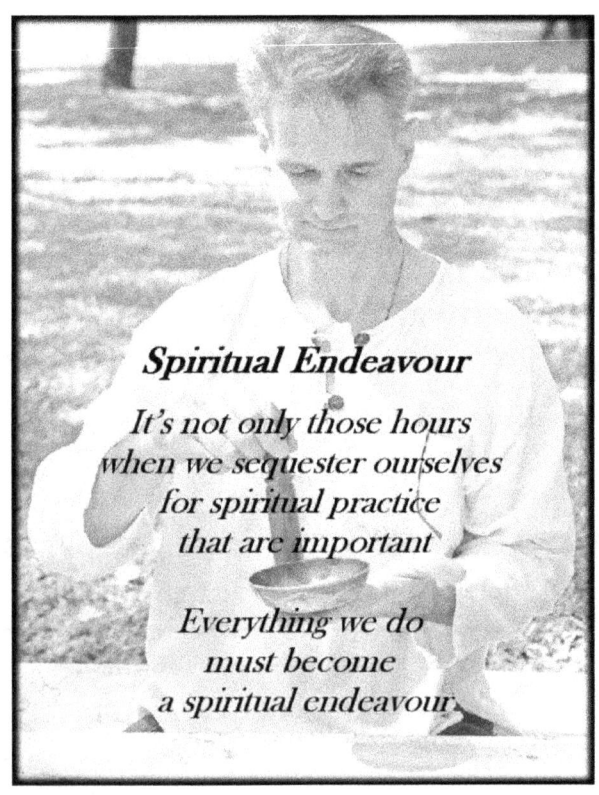

*Spiritual Endeavour*

*It's not only those hours when we sequester ourselves for spiritual practice that are important*

*Everything we do must become a spiritual endeavour*

# Chapter Five

# Reiki 2 Symbols and Procedures

Reiki 2 is a major step forward in your development as a healer and in terms of personal spiritual evolution. The major differences you experience in Reiki 2 include a dramatic increase in energy and increased sensitivity to energy flow. These changes are accompanied by clearer intuition and awareness of the presence of Reiki guidance. A lot of people think that Reiki 2 just means more power. Much more importantly, you may experience profound personal changes in your behaviour, beliefs and attitudes. Channelling Reiki contributes to releasing obsolete patterns of thought and liberating emotional restrictions. Attunement into higher levels of Reiki involves dealing with your self honestly and directly. It may embody surrender and exposure to the roughest qualities of your ego and soul. This is authentic opening and initiation. The process can be very challenging and demanding.

Similarly, channelling Reiki 2 can facilitate and necessitate physical changes. This can be described as a detoxification process as your body begins demanding purer and more ethical sources of food. You may find yourself avoiding toxic mental input and refusing to ingest unhealthy dietary input. You may find it necessary to terminate unhealthy relationships or alter your job situation. Ultimately, the whole process is intensely rewarding, allowing you to grow to your full potential.

Reiki 2 involves the use of three symbols. It includes advanced healing techniques and thorough study of the chakra system. As we evolve spiritually, we become stronger and more sensitive healers for the benefit of all. Most students begin inquiring about Reiki 2 even before they complete Reiki 1. This reveals a natural enthusiasm for a beautiful healing experience. Please be sure you are well established in the foundation practices of Reiki 1 such as hand positions, knowledge of chakras, meditation and mindfulness training before embarking on Reiki 2.

I suggest at least three to six months of regular practice and study of Reiki 1 before proceeding to Reiki 2. It's disheartening to hear of teachers who provide Reiki 1 and 2 training all in one weekend or in one quick week. Evaluate for yourself which training schedule or curriculum best responds to your needs for personal healing and transformation. Reflect honestly on your motivation and needs for Reiki as you decide how to most effectively pursue your training.

On the surface, the healing techniques and procedures in Reiki 1 and 2 are basically the same. The difference resides in your level of intuition, compassion and wisdom. These are the essence of advanced Reiki and they take time to develop. This is why it is basically meaningless to cram Reiki 1 and 2 into a short intensive course; intuition, compassion and wisdom can barely evolve in a week.

## Attunement to Reiki 2

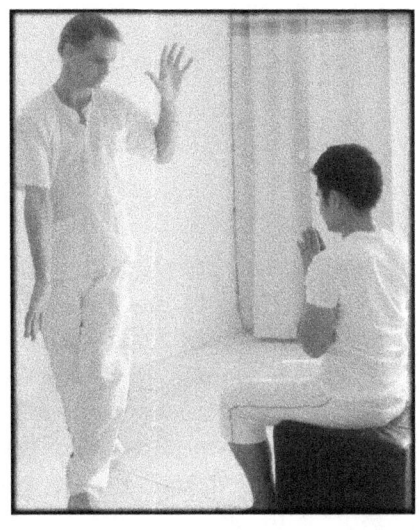

An attunement by a qualified Reiki Master is required to gain access to the energy of Reiki 2. The teacher prepares the training area through a process of purification in which you may assist. The purification includes the use of Reiki symbols, incense, candles, physical cleaning of room, washing hands and feet, meditation and other procedures that are appropriate under the circumstances. The Reiki Master performs a sacred ceremony similar to the one you experienced in Reiki 1. The ceremony is a request for Reiki to attune you to receive symbols, energy, protection, awareness of Reiki guides and stronger intuition.

The attunement process opens you to a profound experience of energy and spirit. Students often perceive colours surrounding the master or around the healing area. Intuition sharply increases with Reiki 2. You may experience this intuition as feelings, as an inner voice of wisdom or as visions that guide you. Reiki spirit guides may also manifest, which you may experience as an additional presence during healings, or visually see, depending on your level of psychic perception. For example, when I performed a distance attunement for Ninfa, she later described how she saw our healing room full of violet colour and perceived an angelic presence during her attunement, which she received at her home in Bolivia 19,000 kilometres (12,000 miles) away from Bangkok! She wrote this about her experience:

My dear Tom,

I would love to share one of the best experiences that I had with Rei Ki. The initiation with you to level 2 was great. I could feel the energy running around me and the energy around my whole place was just flowing like fresh wind inside and outside. I felt at one with the energy flowing...

I treasure this experience and will always be grateful that you let me be part of Rei Ki experience!!! Peaceful Reiki is deep inside me thanks to you! ...What I did not write before is that I could see the symbols in my mind before knowing them from your manual! Your friendship is the best gift that you can give me plus the light that you sent me across the ocean.

Lots of Love,

Ninfa!!!

## Reiki Symbols

Three symbols are studied in Reiki 2. Each symbol is placed into the student's crown to invoke and activate the flow of energy. The most powerful aspect of Reiki 2 is embodied in the use of Reiki symbols to accomplish healing. These symbols were realised by Dr. Usui during his 21 day meditation fast. Some researchers have traced these symbols, and hundreds of others, back to ancient Tibetan healing traditions that were in use between 2000 and 3000 years ago.

Although you may find variations in the symbols in other texts, the purpose and character of each symbol remains the same. Please honour the sacredness of these symbols. Although they are no longer kept secret as was the case through most of history, it is best to regard them with the highest esteem. Please do not leave pictures of the symbols laying about carelessly. Please do not reveal them to those who are unable to share your respect for the sacred.

The symbols are used in numerous situations during healing and meditation sessions. The following suggestions provide basic guidelines for using them. Follow these procedures as much as possible. Remember to touch your tongue to the roof of your mouth whenever you activate the symbols. This connects the two major energy channels of the body. As you gain experience with Reiki 2, you will intuitively know how to use the symbols.

The symbols are used on every chakra during every healing! Visualise the symbols coming in through your crown chakra down to your heart; emanating from your heart through your arms and out your palm chakras. Intend and visualise the symbols entering your patient's chakras, penetrating deeply to the core of their being. This completes a sacred universal connection between all beings and generates deeper compassion and connection between you, your patient and the universe.

**Drawing and Visualising Symbols**

At first, practise drawing the symbols on paper until they become familiar to you and you memorise them. Draw them as large or small as you like. To activate a symbol, tap it with your hand three times while verbalising the name of the symbol. Once you are accurate and confident drawing the symbols with pen and paper, trace the symbols into your palm chakras using your index finger. Draw each symbol and tap it three times as described above.

Another way to use the symbols is by using your palm chakra to draw the symbols in the air. After drawing, clap your hands on the symbol as it "hovers" in the air while reciting its name aloud. This activates the symbol in the room and in your hands. Project the symbols from your palm chakra onto each of the surfaces of the room for purification and protection. As you become more familiar with the symbols, silently visualise them in your mind. With your eyes closed, imagine drawing the symbols. Imagine the symbols any size you like, as small as a cell or as large as the world. Choose the colour of the symbols or let colours arise naturally in your visualisation. Mentally transmit the symbol deeply into the chakras or to the core of anything that you aim to heal.

At first, it may be necessary to draw each individual stroke of the symbols. In time, you will find the symbols appear in your mind in their complete form. As always, say the name of the symbol (silently or aloud) three times to activate it, feeling the sacred sound of each symbol as you vocalise. As you become more proficient with the drawing and visualising of symbols, you will be able to send them anywhere at will. This is most effective in distance healing sessions or sending the symbols into remote areas that require healing. Finally, you can meditate on the symbols and receive guidance and insight into their use.

## Cho Ku Rei: The Power Symbol

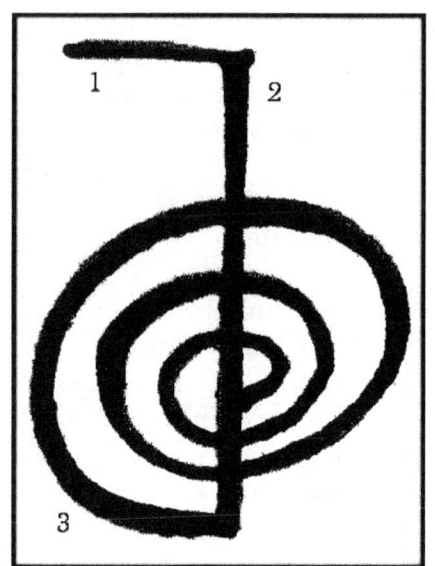

The first symbol in Reiki 2 is Cho Ku Rei (CKR). This symbol greatly increases the power of the Reiki that you channel. Initially, you will consciously invoke this symbol at each chakra and anytime you want to establish protection. As your intuition develops, CKR will automatically arise in your consciousness as needed. At first, please be very diligent about drawing, visualising and invoking this symbol. With practice, it will become familiar and automatic for you.

According to Diane Stein, the line on the top of CKR depicts Shiva (male energy of the universe). The vertical line represents energy emanating from heaven to earth. The spirals represent Shakti (Goddess energy). Note that the spirals touch the diagonal line a total of seven times, corresponding to the seven chakras. Begin drawing the symbol from the top left (1), followed by a downward stroke (2). This is followed by a series of three clockwise spirals crossing the vertical line (3).

When conducting healings with Reiki 2, ask your patients if they have any physical ailments they would like to heal. Discussing those issues helps you focus the intent of CKR. As your patient describes their physical symptoms, your attention and intention focus specifically on those symptoms. The characteristics of CKR can be summarised as follows:

- Increase power
- Protect your chakras
- Focus on physical healing
- Protection on walls, aura and other locations
- Empower water, food and plants
- Energise crystals

## Cho Ku Rei (anti-clockwise)

Alternatively, the orbits of Cho Ku Rei can be drawn anti-clockwise. Generally, the function is the same as with the clockwise symbol. In the early stages of your Reiki 2 training, practise using the symbol in both directions until your intuition guides you to know which one is most appropriate at any given time. The anti-clockwise CKR is used to disperse energy, remove negativity from cysts and remove negativity from auras. Finally, you can use it to ground the soles of the feet.

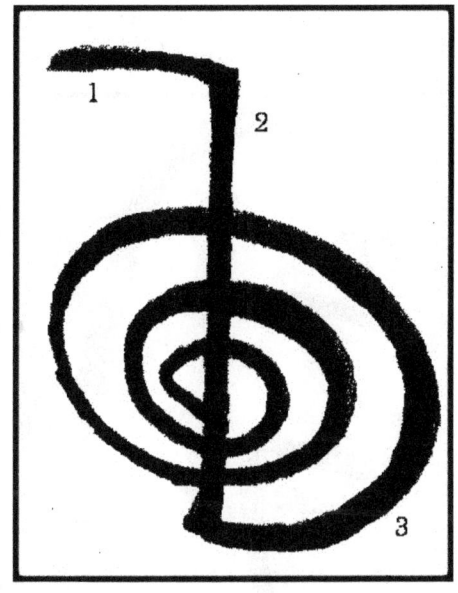

Ultimately, your intention during a healing is of paramount importance. The universal intelligence of Reiki conducts energy through you as a channel. So, rather than intellectualising and labouring over your techniques, just relax and let Reiki flow. Many students try too hard and push the energy, exhausting themselves in the process.

## Sei He Ki: The Emotional Symbol

The second symbol in Reiki 2 is Sei He Ki (SHK). This symbol focuses on emotional issues and purification. During healings, you may be inspired to ask your patient questions. Follow your intuition and you will know what to ask. SHK helps patients release negative emotions. Combining the power of SHK with well-timed, compassionate questions creates a powerful synergy between Western psychological practices and Eastern energy disciplines. Begin with general questions such as, "are there any emotional issues on your mind that you would like to heal? Are there any situations in your life that you would like to overcome?" More specific questions will intuitively arise of their own accord. This subject is discussed in more detail in the section on therapeutic communication, below.

Some sources define SHK as "God and humanity become one." The SHK symbol resembles the two sides of the human brain.

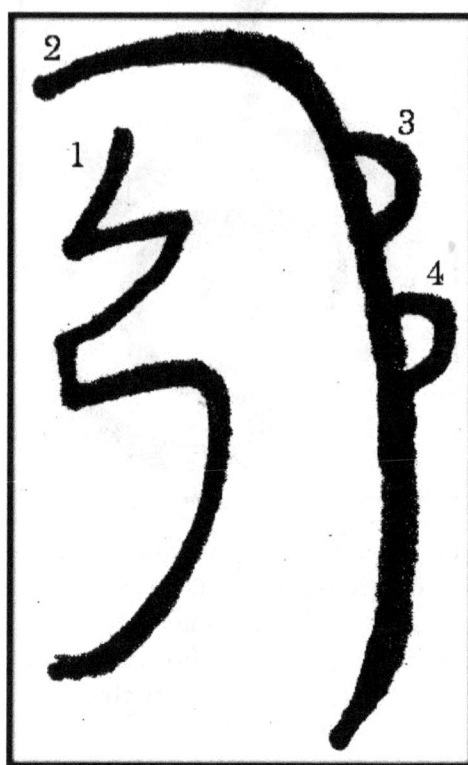

The left side combines angles with straight lines, representing the left side of the human brain, being logical and linear. The right side is curving, representing human creativity and imagination. Draw the symbol beginning with the left side from the top (1). Then draw the right curving line beginning from the top (2). Conclude drawing the symbol by making the small curved marks (3 and 4). As you gain experience with SHK you will comprehend for yourself its esoteric meaning and how to apply it in healing situations. The primary characteristics and uses of SHK can be summarised as follows:

- Use for emotional healing
- Balance the left and right sides of the brain
- Create calmness during stressful situations
- Release stress from its origin
- Purify chakras, rooms and auras
- Purify food, water, plants and crystals
- Release bad habits

# Hon Sha Ze Sho Nen: The Distance Symbol

Hon Sha Ze Sho Nen (HSZ) is the most complex of the Reiki 2 symbols. It can be defined as "No past, no present, no future." Daidi, one of my Reiki students from Taiwan, told me that in Chinese, this symbol can be translated as "Root is the mind," suggesting that the root of all issues is in the mind, in the here and now. As you practise Reiki, you may experience a sense of timelessness that transcends orthodox concepts of time. Reiki allows us to transcend time, to enter the past, present or future (as conceived in orthodox thought). Each occasion during which I transcend time, I realise that "transcend time" is actually a misnomer; past, present and future are concepts, rather than objective facts. For Reiki to be understood, belief in linear time must be transcended and perceived from the perspective of now as eternity; all time is one moment; life is eternally

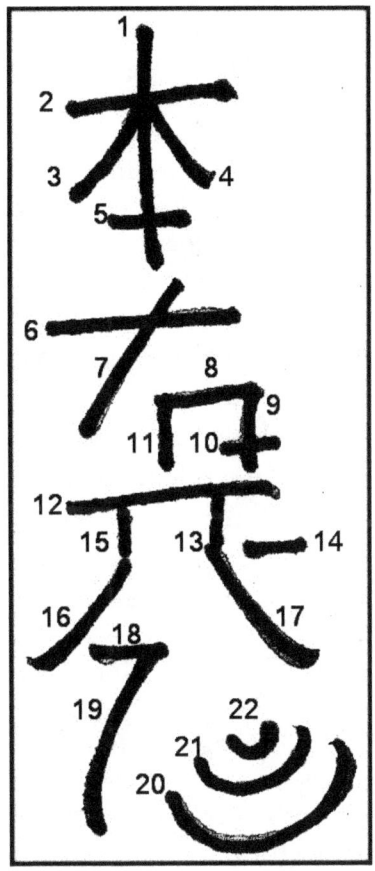

now. If you were wondering why I included a section on quantum physics in chapter one, HSZ is the reason! This symbol gives you the power to prove to yourself that all is one and that separation in terms of time and location is an illusion.

As you practise distance healing with friends, family and other Reiki healers, you'll see for yourself that thought "travels" much faster than light; thought is instantaneous. I remember the very first time that Carol, my Reiki 2 teacher, sent me distance healing. I was feeling really down one night, having trouble processing some of the issues that were arising in my heart during Reiki and meditation; to be honest, I was completely out of it. Carol called that evening, somehow sensing that I was in need of Reiki. We agreed on a ten o'clock healing. I lay down on the sofa and at exactly ten p.m. my feet started buzzing. I was startled to say the least. Within a very short time, I felt very well grounded and deeply peaceful. That was the first of many very powerful distance healing experiences that confirm again and again the interconnectivity of all beings, the power of consciousness and the ability of Reiki to reach across time and distance to its intended destination.

The diagram shows HSZ along with numbers to indicate the order in which to draw the lines. Each mark is drawn beginning from the top or the left. Practise drawing this symbol frequently to assure that you memorise it accurately. The principal uses and characteristics of HSZ can be summarised as follows:

- Heals the conscious mind
- Heals the sub-conscious mind
- Heals the mental body
- Builds a bridge for transmitting distance healing (see chapter six)
- Heals the past
- Used for Karmic healing
- Enhances the future (see chapter six)

**Hands-on Healing with Reiki 2**

When healing with Reiki 2, you are transmitting higher energy, developing as a channel, gaining deeper intuition and tuning into your patient's energies and thoughts. The following section guides you through your healings to be sure you include all the essential steps for the well being of you and your patient.

Preparation for a Reiki 2 session includes all of the steps from Reiki 1, plus use of the symbols. As in Reiki 1, cleanse your healing room with incense or candles. Sitting in meditation for 15 to 20 minutes before your patient arrives will help you centre and ground yourself. During your meditation, visualise the Reiki symbols around you. Draw or visualise SHK to purify the walls, ceiling, floor and healing surface. Draw or visualise CKR to protect walls, ceiling, floor and healing surface. Remember to recite the name of each symbol three times. Finally, draw or visualise HSZ to focus your mind on the healing process. Some people also like to draw all three symbols on their hands prior to healing. As an added measure of protection and purity, visualise white light all around you.

Confirm your patient's permission and willingness to receive the healing. Discuss the healing process as you would in Reiki 1, plus bringing up any issues that you intuitively sense may be important during the session. Ask which mental, emotional or physical issues your patient would like to resolve. Be sure that you make it clear that Reiki is "co-healing" between Reiki, healer and patient; the patient needs to invest time, energy and effort to improve their own health. Ask which changes they are willing to make to improve their well-being.

### The Healing Process

Sweep your hands through your patient's aura and scan their energy. Determine if the healing should begin at the crown or at the feet. If in doubt, simply ask your "inner guide" for guidance. The complete healing includes the feet, knees and the seven major chakras just as in Reiki 1. At each location, your hands will sense whether or not you should make physical contact or keep a slight distance away from the body. In Reiki 2, visualise all three symbols flowing into every chakra. The symbols help you maintain focus on the healing process and strengthen your intent. Discussion during the healing is used in conjunction with knowledge of chakras, sensations in your hands and your patient's verbal input to the healing procedure. This is where therapeutic communication becomes very important.

### Therapeutic Communication

Conversation with your patient is a powerful aspect of Reiki. While receiving Reiki, patients tend to be more relaxed and open to discussion. During the healing process you can ask questions to nurture your patient's healing growth. This is conducive to helping them make important changes in their lives. Each communication has a unique flavour; some patients talk the entire time while others remain silent. Initiate conversation before healing begins to assess the direction of the session. If your patient becomes very still and taciturn during the healing, respect their silence and save the discussion for later.

Effective communication is as important as the ability to channel energy. Healing involves helping a patient see, honour and release energetic patterns that are no longer constructive. As a healer, you can help a patient perceive the relationship between their emotions, beliefs and physical ailments so they gain a fresh perspective to evaluate their lives. Gently assist them in gaining personal insight. This is a co-creative process between Reiki, healer and patient.

Many of the suggestions described in this section echo the teachings of an ancient Tibetan Shaman named Wei Chi published in "The Lost Steps of Reiki, the Channelled Teachings of Wei Chi." His original teachings have been channelled in recent times and include many concepts that are not generally included in Reiki classes. The Wei Chi system focuses on dialogue between healer and client. Each person must acknowledge their own participation and obligation to heal themself. The healer receives information to benefit the client, in addition to healing energy. In my experience, information arises in many healings, including suggestions concerning nutrition, exercise and hidden issues of the heart. Using the suggestions of Wei Chi, the Reiki system is more interactive, a form of co-healing rather than a hierarchical doctor-patient relationship.

Here are a few sample questions that you might raise during healing sessions. More importantly, listen to your own intuition and you will know which topics need to be addressed.

- What outcome would you like from this healing? Can you visualise that?
- What is the exact question that you would like to answer?
- What is the exact problem that you want to overcome?
- Are you willing to make changes to achieve that outcome?

For example, one evening I was sending Reiki by distance to my friend Flo when she was in Argentina. While healing her root chakra, I saw an image in my mind of an older man. Knowing the chakra system, I suspected that this image related to her early relationship with her father. I described my vision in an email to see how Flo would respond to it. She confirmed that she has long term issues with her father that still needed to be resolved.

Some patients may choose to interpret such images, or just listen to your description and reflect on it later. In a hands-on healing, patients may want to discuss the imagery in more detail while others will just nod their heads and fall asleep. In any event, let your patient lead the healing process and interpretation as much as they can. For your part, ask general questions to see how much is on their minds. This is intuitive, therapeutic, energetic co-healing!

When I first met my friend Kwang, she reported having constipation for many years. Despite numerous attempts to solve the situation, her symptoms never improved. My intuition suggested that she was suffering from some blockage related to relationships with her parents. As we discussed her childhood, she cried several very old tears. Later, in response to her healing experience, she wrote,

> I can't remember when I first started to believe that people do indeed forgive. I believe it, but that doesn't mean that I can actually do it. Almost my entire life I've had to endure anguish and resentment caused by my parents. I hadn't realised that all this negativity inside me was connected to my physical well-being. As long as forgiveness challenged me, I continued to have constipation and was addicted to laxatives. The crucial transformation came when I joined a 5 day naturopathy course led by 3 instructors: P' Mai, Tom, and P' Oh. Not only did we learn naturopathy but also received Reiki therapeutic treatment.
>
> While Tom began his Reiki treatment, I told him about my problem with constipation. Surprisingly, he queried me about my life and problems with my mom. It seemed to me that Tom and I just had a good conversation in a relaxing atmosphere; he talked with me and asked a few questions, which led me to recall those relentless problems. In this session, Tom was sending his energy to my stomach covering the digestive system. He also sent the Reiki energy through his palms to cover my whole body from head to toes. That day, Tom helped me realise that the problems I had with my mom directly related to constipation: both were awful and ceaseless, and of course, I needed to let go of them.

Five days afterwards, I returned to a normal life in Bangkok. Something miraculous happened during this time: I no longer had constipation! My bowel movements were back to normal. I was no longer under the spell of laxatives. You have no idea how wonderful this is! This small miracle, I believe, came from a combination of adjusting my eating habits, Reiki, Chakra healing and an attempt to ease the anguish between my mom and I.

Oh… the most important thing is about faith and conviction. I have faith in unseen energy. Had I laughed at Reiki when I saw Tom moving his hands I would surely remain addicted to those laxatives. At present, although I barely eat fresh fruit or get exercise, my bowel movements are normal and perhaps excellent. The anguish between my mother and I has not been easily resolved, though. Every day I still must try to come to terms with it hoping that one day it will be unravelled.

Four years have passed since that healing and the constipation has never returned. The physical blockage was completely released by addressing the family issue that troubled her so deeply within her self. It's such a pleasure to see Kwang happy and healthy. She is now watching her nutrition more carefully and she has opened her own Vegan restaurant.

Dr. John Upledger characterises the secret of all effective healing methods as the process of leading a patient to an honest and truthful self-discovery. Self discovery is required for the initiation and continuation of self-healing. He explains that only through self-healing, in contrast to "curing," patients can experience both permanent recovery and spiritual growth. He goes on to say that, "the closer our perception of self approaches the truth, the deeper our capacity for self healing becomes." His notion of healing is very relevant to the practice of Reiki, not only in terms of self healing that we emphasise in Reiki 1, but also in recognising our responsibility and role in facilitating the true growth of our patients. Keep in mind, when you are healing another person, in fact, you are facilitating their self healing. The aim is to support them to accept their duty and responsibility for their own growth. Once you help them back on their feet, they can take steps on their own.

## Sending Reiki to the Origin of Issues

During healings, request Reiki to heal the origin of any emotional, mental, physical or spiritual issue. This includes childhood traumas, or even a situation from a previous or parallel existence (which transcend orthodox human comprehension). Use Hon Sha Ze Sho Nen to connect to the origin of the issue and ask the energy to heal the root of the issue. After all, the root of all issues is in the present mind. You may have read about people trying to heal their Karma. In simplest terms, Karma translates as action: Every action and every thought that we conceive is the result of some previous action, as well as the cause of some future experience.

    I consider Karma to be the great equilibrium of life. Karma does not dictate events or results; rather, it balances the energies of all beings and all events. To me, Karma works like a billion flasks of protons, electrons and neutrons that naturally charge or neutralise each other while seeking universal balance. Karma, at the level of energy, seeks universal equilibrium. On the surface, it may appear to manifest as phenomena such as good luck, bad luck and coincidence.

    How can we reconcile our understanding of Karma with destiny and free will? Destiny, like Karma, does not dictate. Rather, destiny or Karma seek balance by equalising all energies vis-à-vis other beings. Within this flexible framework of equalising energies rather than dictating results, free will can still be exercised. We make choices from various options. The point is that each choice is tethered within the bounds of our energetic essence. This means that all free choices are made from within a range of options available to us as prescribed by our Karmic assets or debt.

    Working with Karma can be very serious, intensive and complex. It should be pursued only after you have made significant progress as a healer. When you are ready, seek the guidance of an experienced Karmic healer. For present purposes, simply ask Reiki to heal at the source of an issue, whether that is in the past, present or future.

## Closing the Healing Process

Completion of a Reiki 2 healing session includes all the steps that you practised in Reiki 1, including sweeping your hands through the aura, balancing the chakras and closing the aura. When closing the aura, visualise the Reiki 2 symbols in a "cocoon" surrounding the patient to protect, purify and seal the healing. You may also request that the healing repeat at a specific time in the future.

While thanking Reiki with blessings and thoughts of gratitude, I often request Reiki to conduct subsequent healing at the time my patient goes to bed on the next night. In some cases, I ask Reiki to repeat every night for the following week. I simply listen to my intuition to know the best prescription for repeat healings. Requesting subsequent healings follows the process described in the distance healing section in chapter six.

## After Healing is Complete

As always, thank Reiki for the healing. Sweep energy out of your aura to be sure no energies are attached. Use the symbols to cleanse yourself as necessary. Discuss any insights or questions that arose during the healing, which may be more detailed than what you experienced with Reiki 1. Since you are channelling more energy with Reiki 2, your patient is experiencing a more profound and radical healing experience. Be sure they are well grounded before they leave. If necessary, place your hands on their feet for a few more minutes to bring them fully into their bodies. Finally, discuss the potential detoxification process that may follow a healing. The detoxification may be more intense than what you triggered with your Reiki 1 healings. Remind the patient that any minor symptoms that arise in the next few days such as diarrhoea, sweating or sleepiness are indicative of the energy flowing through the body and mind, cleansing away outdated thoughts, feelings and cells, bringing new vitality to their whole being.

These natural detoxification processes of the body are to be welcomed and encouraged and should not be suppressed. If your patient calls you the next day to report having a fever, please encourage them to take the day off of work, stay in bed, drink plenty of liquids and avoid taking any chemical medicine. Encourage them to know and trust their body's innate healing mechanism to rid itself of unwanted matter and energy.

This concludes the basic procedures and concepts that you need when first learning Reiki 2. The following chapter presents the next stage of your development as a healer by conducting distance healings and working more profoundly on your personal past. Please continue to practise self healing and meditation every day as you embark on these advanced steps.

It is not posture or prayer,
But awareness and intent,
That are essential to the soul

# Chapter Six

# Advanced Reiki 2

Once you know and understand the use of symbols in Reiki 2, you can move on to more advanced healing and transformational experiences. The most fascinating aspect of Reiki 2 for most people is the ability to conduct distance healings. These healings transcend time, allowing you to direct energy into the past, present or future. You can send distance healing real-time or arrange it to arrive at a time agreed on with the recipient. You can also request Reiki to repeat any number of times in the coming days.

# Distance Healing

I started doing Reiki by distance in 2005. Meena called saying she was very stressed with her exams and she couldn't sleep. We arranged a distance Reiki session and agreed to follow up a few days later. To our mutual delight, she reported sleeping very soundly and faced her exams with much greater confidence and no more sense of dread. I realised that by sending Reiki across Bangkok to a friend on the other side of the river was a very real event. This indicated that my usual perception of time and space was not quite accurate.

As you practise this technique, you soon realise that concepts of time; past, present and future, are illusions. For me, this was the most astonishing insight that came from practising distance healing. It's nearly impossible to explain this to somebody who has never experienced it. My orthodox concept of linear time simply didn't hold up any longer after the visceral experience of transcending time and space with Reiki. Through subsequent reading, I learned that my experience with distance healing was totally consistent with the principles of quantum physics. In fact, distance healing with Reiki has inspired my passion for studying quantum physics in recent years.

Distance healing was my first solid experience of my consciousness influencing another person at a remote location. Strangely enough, quantum physicists struggled for ages to recognise and accept that they were influencing the results of their experiments through the very act of observation. Initially, the influence of the quantum observer seemed to be a barrier to "pure objective science." Finally, quantum physicists recognised that consciousness not only influences matter, but consciousness is essential to nature. To think that human consciousness is somehow separate from nature is a fallacy rooted in antiquated classical science. Nature is conscious!

When a physicist observes quantum behaviour, quantum particles respond to their attention. The consciousness of the quantum observer influences sub-atomic behaviour in the same way that the consciousness of a Reiki healer influences the energy and health of a patient. Our minds are constituent parts of the universe, influencing not only each other, but also water, plants, trees and sub-atomic particles.

Luckily, you don't need to be a quantum physicist in order to send distance Reiki healing! Are you ready to try it yourself and prove the power of Reiki and consciousness through your own experience?

Remember, you need to be attuned by a qualified Reiki master to empower you to pursue this practice. The distance healing process includes the following steps:

- Purify your healing area
- Receive permission from the recipient to send the healing (personally or psychically)
- Sit quietly in a meditative state free from any disturbances
- Mentally purify the area where the person is receiving the healing using Reiki symbols
- Visualise the person and make psychic contact with them
- Mentally perform each of the procedures as in a hands-on healing session
- Alternatively, hold a photograph in your hands to assist the visualisation process
- If you like, use your own knee or leg as a "representative" of the person receiving the healing; move your hands according to the healing positions that you are visualising
- Close the distance healing process by mentally following the procedures as in hands-on healing
- Follow up with your patient to discuss any insights, questions or phenomena that arise during the healing

Remain mindful throughout the distance healing session. If you feel any illness or pain in your body coming from your patient, mentally remove yourself from the situation for a moment. Collect your thoughts and re-affirm that you are sending energy one-way, and not collecting any negativity from the session.

## Distance Healing to your Younger Self

Train yourself in distance healing by working with your self. Rather than doing self healings as you did with Reiki 1, now you can send Reiki to yourself "by distance." Use distance healing to heal issues in your own life. Sit down in your healing room, let's say, at 9:00 p.m. Meditate long enough to clear your mind, relax your body and establish concentration. Visualise yourself lying in bed at 10:00 p.m.

and send energy to your "distant self." By visualising yourself in a different room at a different time, you "bend" time and space.

When you physically lie down in bed at 10:00 p.m., observe any sensations that indicate the flow of Reiki arriving. The further test will be to see how well you sleep and how you feel in the morning. Once you are familiar with sending distance healing to yourself, practise sending Reiki to other Reiki healers who understand the process. As you gain experience, begin sharing distance Reiki with friends and family. Use photographs, written notes or visualisation to facilitate the healing process.

The most powerful training procedure that I teach in Reiki 2 is to have students send distance healing to their "younger self." This process may require several months, healing one year of life at a time. If for example you are now 32 years old, send energy back to yourself when you were 31 years old. During your next session, send Reiki back to when you were 30 years old. Ultimately, send Reiki to your very birth and beyond. If the process becomes too intense, slow down and take a few days off. There's no hurry! You've taken a lifetime to accumulate your issues; you don't need to discard them all this week. Each healing session focuses on one year of life at a time. Set a pace at which you can comfortably address your past, bring it into your present consciousness and allow Reiki to help you reconcile any outstanding issues. Be sure to keep notes throughout the healing process.

When Daidi completed her Reiki 2 training, she began exploring India and Thailand. As part of her Reiki 2 training, she sent distance healing to herself for every year of her life. She wrote,

> Reiki changed my life, even better, it changed my attitude towards life. First of all, it helped me re-organise my life in learning how to treat and love my body in the right way when I'm losing control over it. To heal myself physically has been always a process of learning to realise that we need constant care and awareness of ourselves. Reiki helped me appreciate living in a simple and healthy way through connecting with nature more and always maintaining a positive mind.
>
> Reiki teaches me to respect myself and others as we are. It shows me how our spirits relate to our body and mind. Reiki helped me realise that life is literally a holistic journey. Eventually, I realised that it was not merely the place where I live that matters, but the positive concept to live, grow and continually learn to be at ONENESS with our universe. I learned to

dedicate my talents in creating artwork, writing and translating, spreading positive energy to more people and to benefit humanity.

## Healing and Manifesting through Written Request

It's very powerful to write down your request to focus your intent during healings and manifestations. The act of writing strengthens your commitment and makes your intention much more concrete. I would like to share a technique that Carol, my Reiki 2 teacher from South Africa, taught me several years ago: Draw a triangle with an open top as shown in the diagram below. Write your request inside the triangle. Use this process for conducting a distance healing session or for manifesting life change.

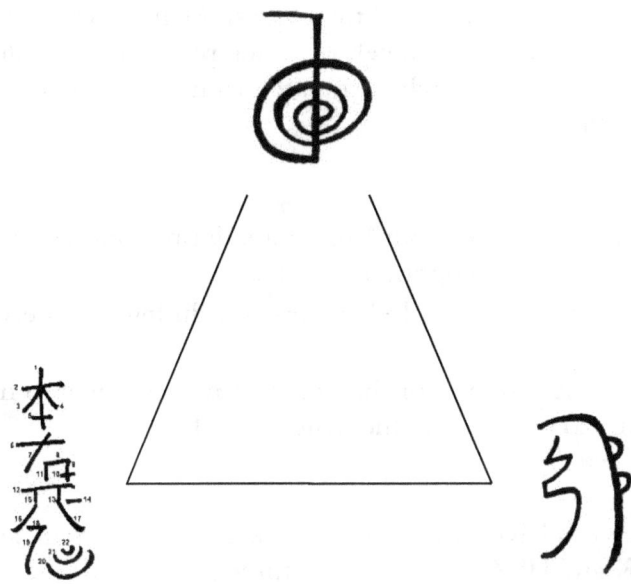

Using Reiki, you have the ability to manifest whatever you need in your life. The energy available in the universe is abundant and available to you for the asking. Use Reiki to manifest those things you need in your life or to support you through an upcoming event. Once you realise that you have a right to abundance and you deserve a good life, then you can graciously open yourself to receive the gifts of the universe. Use these sample sentences to guide you in writing healing or manifestation requests.

- Please heal Maureen at the physical, mental, spiritual and emotional levels.
- Specifically, help reduce her stress, headaches and sore neck at the origin of these problems.
- Please help Maureen gain insight into the causes of her illness and guide her on the path for a strong recovery from all illness.
- Please repeat this healing process on Wednesday and Friday nights at 10.

Manifestation works in the same way as healing. By manifestation, I mean to contribute to a future event by invoking the power of Reiki for support. The only difference between healing and manifestation is the content of the request. Manifestation refers to events such as interviews, travels or facing professional challenges. Consider these examples when you are manifesting either for yourself or for another person.

- Please let Reiki flow from 1 to 3 p.m. during June's exam on Monday to achieve optimum results.
- Please support June to do her very best during her interview on Friday at 5:00 p.m.
- I request these things, or their equivalent, according to free will, harming no one and for the benefit of all.

Once you have written your request inside the triangle, draw CKR, SHK and HSZ symbols at the three points of the triangle. Draw CKR for empowerment, followed by SHK for emotional focus and HSZ for mental focus. Sign the paper, fold it and hold it between your hands. Meditate, sending Reiki to the request and visualising the request taking place as you intend it. Similarly, visualise the successful interview or examination that you aim to empower. Consider it done! When making your requests, be sure to follow these steps:

- Be sure that your request will not harm anyone
- Never ask for something that would deprive others
- Be careful not to violate the free will of another person
- Do not ask for a specific job or relationship; rather, request the job or relationship that is most suitable for you
- Believe in your right to abundance
- Thank Reiki for supporting your request
- Meditate, seeing the fulfilment of your request
- Afterwards, place the request under a lit candle or a crystal
- Then, let it go; release all expectations

As you will soon experience, Reiki works in the past, present and future with equal efficiency. Practise each of these techniques until they become a familiar and natural path to your personal transformation. I trust you will find these approaches to be very empowering!

## Self Knowledge

Self knowledge means knowing all parts of ourselves, even the parts we do not like. Just accept that you have those parts, and gently work on your self. Be aware that what you don't like in others may reflect some aspect of your shadow self.

Another dimension of self knowledge is that your body stores emotional experience. This means that pain in your body reflects pain in your emotions. You may find that Yoga is needed to release from the body what meditation releases from the mind. Include Yoga meditation and asanas (postures) in your daily training in addition to sitting meditation and continuous mindfulness throughout the day.

Mindfulness nourishes greater awareness of anxiety and helps you become conscious of your own creation of limiting beliefs. The following questions are included to guide you to know your true self as you create yourself moment by moment, thought by thought. Only you can ask, only you can answer, and only you can know. Reflect on each of these questions and see which ones resonate with you, positively or negatively, as indication of need for changes in your thoughts and beliefs about yourself.

1. To what extent do I blame others for doing what I myself exhibit, but hide from myself?
2. Are my critiques of others more accurately read as an indictment of my own shadow self?
3. Before condemning her, would it be more effective to identify my own flaws?

## Personal Insight through Reiki

Use Reiki to discover answers to your most perplexing questions and solutions to your most challenging situations. The Reiki experience is exemplified by one of my students who has studied both Reiki 2 and Reiki 3 with me. She writes,

> I am Dilhara from Sri Lanka. I come from a difficult family background and growing up I always believed that I was meant to do something and help others and find myself. I had problems with self esteem and could not fully believe that I could set goals or achieve them. I had a great opportunity to do Reiki 1 Training. It was a great experience and I knew that this was my calling. During the next few months I moved countries and finally was able to achieve my goal in becoming a therapist.
>
> My experience of Reiki 2 was amazing and gave me such a positive outlook on life and everything around me. I love my job, my apartment and now looking forward to a promotion as a supervisor. I have achieved my dream of buying my own land. I continued my final stage in becoming a Reiki Master and successfully achieved that with my master Tom Radzienda.
>
> One last challenge in my life that I needed to do was to stop smoking and I have finally managed to accomplish this! I feel at peace with myself and find by sharing my gift of Reiki Universal energy I am able to help others and feel more complete. I feel in control of my life and take every day and every opportunity as a blessing and I'm grateful for this Great experience.

To gain insight into your personal situation, draw the open triangle as shown above. Write the exact question that you would like to address. Here are a few life changing questions and requests to guide you in your growth through Reiki:

- What do I really want from life?
- What is the most suitable method for my personal development?
- What is the ultimate source of my wisdom?
- Where is my true value?
- Please increase the flow of Reiki to deepen my spiritual awareness
- Please deepen my meditation practice
- Please send Reiki to support me to prioritise my life
- Please show me how to best develop myself for the benefit of all beings

Draw the symbols on the paper and hold it between your hands. Meditate on your question and listen to your intuition for answers. Sit quietly and allow the answers to rise from the silence.

To round out this chapter on Reiki 2, I would like to include an explanation of pendulums and crystals that will further enhance your healing practice.

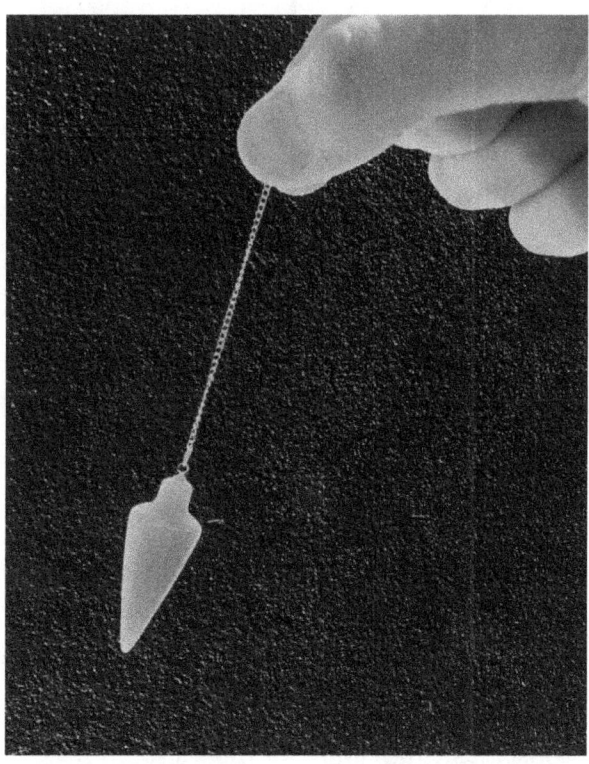

## Using a Pendulum with Reiki

What is a pendulum? A pendulum is a cone-shaped crystal suspended on a fine silver chain. It swings in response to fluctuations in the muscles and amplifies these to make them more apparent.

How does it work? The human body responds to subtle energy from the environment and passes this information to the subconscious. Consequently, the muscles respond at a very minute level. A pendulum reflects this muscular activity by swinging or circling in response to the energies being experienced. Using a pendulum during healings is very helpful for diagnosing issues and confirming your intuition.

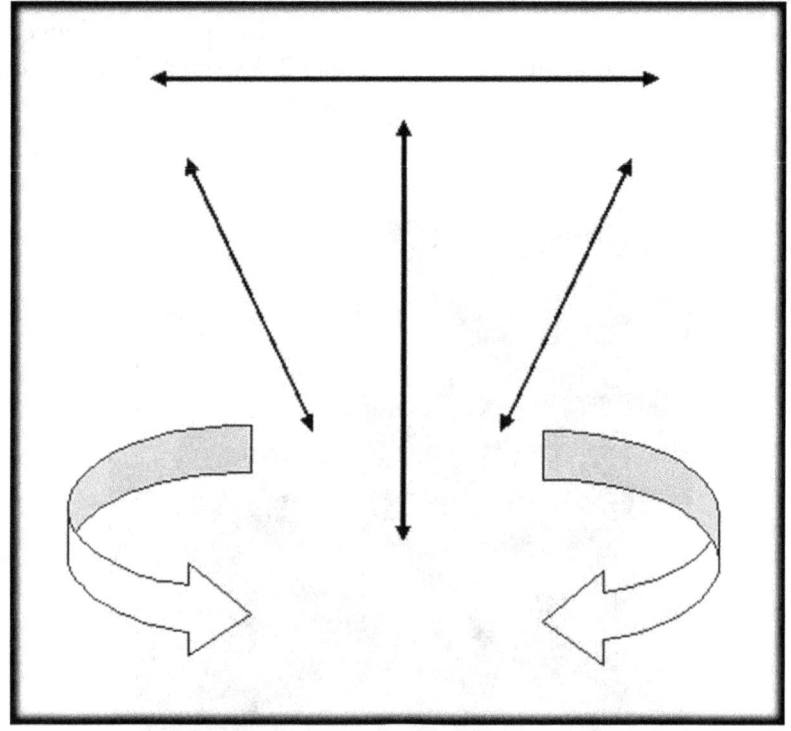

How can I make it move? To use your pendulum, sit very still in a relaxed, meditative state. Allow the pendulum to hang freely from your fingertips and mentally intend it to begin tracing over the arrows in the diagram above. With practice and patience, your pendulum will swing by itself, by mentally intending to make it move, but without consciously moving your muscles.

Practise further by mentally intending it to swing in clockwise and anti-clockwise circles. I remember when Sabrina first saw me using a pendulum during her healing session. She was so fascinated that she went and immediately purchased a pendulum for her own use. She marvelled at the simplicity and beauty of a pendulum reading energy and the insights it could indicate.

## Calibrating your Pendulum

|  | Direction | Confirm |
|---|---|---|
| Yes |  |  |
| No |  |  |
| No information possible |  |  |
| Positive |  |  |
| Negative |  |  |
| Neutral |  |  |

Once your pendulum is moving freely by intention alone, begin asking questions and making requests to see what the pendulum will show you of its own accord. Request your pendulum to indicate the direction of "yes," until a definite direction can be perceived. Then, request it to demonstrate the direction of "no" until it is clearly indicated. Request the pendulum to illustrate "no information possible," "positive," "negative" and "neutral" until all indications are clear. The pendulum will swing in a straight line or move in circles by itself. For some people, "yes" may be indicated by a clockwise circle, whereas for other people "yes" is indicated by swinging in a horizontal line. For me, my pendulum indicates "yes" by swinging in a line between 10 o'clock and 4 o'clock on the face of a clock. Most importantly, avoid expectations of which way the pendulum "should" swing and just allow it to move naturally.

Go back to the beginning and check all responses again and again until you are confident that the responses are accurate and consistent. Fill in the chart on the previous page as you determine the indications of your personal pendulum. In a few weeks, check it again to confirm that your readings are accurate and stable.

### Reading with your Pendulum

Relax in a non-thinking mode, with only positive motives. Begin reading with your pendulum by asking some basic questions such as: "Is this shirt blue? Is today Thursday?" Ask a series of yes/no questions until you get steadily accurate readings. Properly phrased questions are essential to the accuracy of your pendulum.

For another example, think of a place that you are considering visiting and hold that image in your mind. Ask in your heart, "Is it a good idea for me to go there? Is Saturday the best day for me to go? Will my project there be successful?" By asking a series of yes/no questions, you can receive complex answers. Keep your questions simple. Avoid using compound sentences or negative words such as "can't, won't and don't."

Proceed to ask questions such as, "Is the energy of this crystal positive or negative for me? How does this job resonate with me?" Further practice can include a wider variety of situations. For example, pick up a piece of food, hold it to your solar plexus and ask, "Is this food positive or negative for me?" You can even do this at the supermarket while shopping if you don't mind a few customers staring at you in wonder. Additionally, try holding photographs or books to your solar plexus and asking the pendulum to indicate the energy of each item. Also experiment with your pendulum by reading Reiki and other symbols. Hold the pendulum over a drawing of a symbol and see what it indicates about the energy of the symbol. Similarly, just visualise the symbol and see what impression you receive from your pendulum.

Confirm your readings by asking, "Is this a true answer? Have my own feelings influenced this answer?" Once you recognise the patterns and answers you get from your pendulum, begin asking more challenging, esoteric questions. For example, begin reading the energy of chakras.

## Reading the Energy of Chakras with a Pendulum

Place your hand on one of your chakras and request the pendulum to show you the quality of energy in that chakra. Repeat this process for all chakras or organs as you determine the positive and negative energies that you encounter during healings.

I use a pendulum during most healing sessions. I place my hand on a person's chakra and ask the pendulum to show the nature of the energy in that chakra. As the healing progresses, I observe the changing motion of the pendulum until it indicates a strongly positive energy flow. Once a chakra is finished, the pendulum gradually slows down to a halt, indicating that it is time to move on to the next chakra.

Indeed, using a pendulum takes time and practice. At first, it may seem that your pendulum hardly moves. With patience, you will soon see it moving. For sure, some doubts will arise during your practice. You may be thinking to yourself that you are purposely making it move using your arm or shoulder. Maybe that's true, so you need to sit extra still and be mindful of your body movements. Sooner or later, you'll be demonstrating your pendulum to a friend and they may raise their own doubts. They may claim that you're moving very slightly or you have some trick in your hands. With practice, your confidence will increase and you will recognise for yourself that by keeping your mind neutral and your body still, your muscles subtly move the pendulum without any conscious effort. This will give you greater insight into the quality of energy in a person's chakras or aura.

## Using Crystals with Reiki

Every time Vipaporn came for her Reiki lesson, she brought more crystals with her. Clearly, she was very attracted to crystals and wanted to incorporate them into her healing practice. On the other hand, some students come into our meditation room and wonder why we have this funny collection of rocks. Once you have learned the basic techniques of Reiki, you are encouraged to learn more about crystals and see if they resonate with you in your healing sessions.

Refer to a book on crystals such as Judy Hall's "Crystal Bible" for complete references about the healing and esoteric qualities of various stones. Crystals can be placed directly on a patient's body, in their hands or within their aura. They can also be used around the house for purification, near your computer to absorb electronic energy, to absorb pollutants and absorb natural radiation. You can strategically place crystals around your house for neutralising geopathic stress and negative environmental energies. Crystals can be worn as jewellery around your neck or carried in your pocket. You can also submerge crystals in drinking water to strengthen and purify it.

I employ crystals in most, but not all of my healing sessions. If I sense that somebody would be sceptical of crystals, I'm much less likely to use them. On the other hand, some patients are really keen on discovering crystals, so I use them more liberally.

At the earth chakra located just below the feet, place a grounding stone such as hematite or smoky quartz. I generally do this during every healing because these stones are helpful for collecting any negative energy swept from the patient's aura during healing. It's especially important to cleanse these stones before and after each healing, as they function as a receptacle for negative or unwanted energy.

Many crystals can be effectively used on each of the chakras. I've included just a few to give you a taste of the variety and diversity of healing stones available to us here on earth. For the root chakra, smoky quartz assists in grounding and purifying. You can also choose a crystal such as red carnelian which is a stabilising stone that promotes self-trust. Red jasper grounds energy and can also be used for healing the digestive and sexual organs. If your patient has specific issues to heal, choose crystals for their specific healing characteristics.

Once again, let me remind you to cleanse your healing crystals after each use. Run them under fresh water or rinse them with salt water. You can also hold them in your hands to energise and purify them. With Reiki 2, visualise the Cho Ku Rei and Sei He Ki symbols penetrating and empowering each stone. Finally, you can place your crystals in the sunshine to gather the energy of the sun and further purify them.

For the navel chakra, choose red jasper for healing of sexual organs and enhancing sexual relationships. Orange calcite effectively balances the emotions, removes fear and helps people overcome depression. It's used for healing the reproductive system, the gall bladder and intestinal disorders such as irritable bowel syndrome. I also use a raw bloodstone quite often, especially for women, to help with blood circulation and menstrual problems.

Over the long term, study a book on crystals and learn the specific qualities of each stone. Purchase those stones that most resonate with you and incorporate them into your healing. Most often, I allow my intuition to select the most suitable stones for each healing. Call it laziness if you must, but I simply bring out my tray of healing stones, let my hand hover over the crystals until I feel naturally inclined to select a few for my patient. Indeed, I'm employing basic knowledge of crystals such as knowing which colour is suitable for each chakra, but I also trust my hand and heart to select stones that resonate with me at that moment.

Yellow tourmaline stimulates the solar plexus and is helpful to enhance personal power. Physically, it treats the stomach, liver, spleen, kidneys and gallbladder. Another beautiful stone is the tiger's eye which works on strengthening self worth, manifesting the will and overcoming self criticism. Generally, crystals of a yellow or golden hue are suitable for placement on the solar plexus chakra.

While scanning your patient's body at the beginning of a healing, you may find a blockage or weakness at one of the chakras. In this case, place the crystal directly on the chakra throughout the healing. The crystal then functions as your "third hand" throughout the duration of the healing process. When doing this, many people report that they feel my hand on that chakra even though I am physically at a different healing location.

I normally place a rose quartz on the heart chakra. The first stone that I fell in love with was a rose quartz and I carried it with me all the time. I used it in practically every healing. Finally, realising that I had grown attached to it, I decided to give it to a good friend. It was the finest gift I had in my possession and sharing it with a close friend was the most important thing I could do with it. Rose quartz symbolises unconditional love, purifying the heart at all levels including love of self. As you strengthen your love of self, you will automatically attract loving relationships into your life. Rhodonite is another pink coloured stone that can be placed directly on the heart chakra, or just above it. Rhodonite heals emotional wounds, facilitates forgiveness and transmutes painful emotions. Green stones such as green tourmaline, green quartz and moss agate can also be used effectively when working on the heart.

It would be very uncomfortable if you placed a crystal directly on the throat. It's better to place your chosen crystals below the throat or to one side. I normally use a blue quartz that I acquired in the mystical town of Capilla del Monte in central Argentina. I use it specifically for healing throat issues. For a long time, this was my personal favourite stone, so I always carried it in my pocket. As I got used to it (and it attuned to me), I felt confident using it in most healings. This shows that confidence in the healing power of a crystal, plus regular association with it, empowers you and your crystals to be more effective at healing.

More recently, I've begun using a lapis lazuli that my wife brought back for me from the sacred mountains of Pushkar in Rajasthan, India last year. I first heard of lapis lazuli in the epic poem by W.B. Yeats where he describes the power of the arts and artisans, which coincidentally relate to the creative aspects of the throat chakra. Although I don't know if Yeats was familiar with the healing qualities of lapis lazuli, he was certainly attracted to the beauty and imaginative characteristics of this visionary stone. Lapis lazuli balances the throat chakra and heals the throat, larynx, thyroid and thymus. It is said to encourage self awareness and strengthen self expression, the major issues of the throat chakra. Lapis makes beautiful jewellery that can attractively and therapeutically be worn around the neck.

On the brow chakra, lapis lazuli can also be used to enhance psychic ability and guide you on your spiritual path. In my own practice, I generally place purple amethyst on the brow during meditation, when healing myself and healing others. My first experience with this crystal was when my friend Ken visited from England. He had been using amethyst in his healing work for decades, and this was the stone he selected as a gift for me. Amethyst has a high spiritual vibration. It strengthens common sense, spiritual insight, intuition and psychic ability. It's always suitable for use on the brow chakra.

Purple amethyst is also useful on the crown chakra because it connects the physical, mental and emotional bodies with the spiritual. It cleanses the aura and transmutes negative energy. Overall, it's one of the most spiritual stones. If I had to recommend a single stone for your healing and meditation practice, I would suggest amethyst.

In some cases, I ask my patients to select by themselves which crystals they would like to use during their healing session. This empowers them to participate more actively in the healing experience. Ask them to place the crystals anywhere on their body where they feel they would like extra healing support.

If you decide to purchase crystals for your own use, visit a gem shop and examine their inventory. Pick up any stone that you find attractive and hold it in your hand to sense its energy. Trust your intuition whether or not the stone resonates well with you. Discuss the qualities of the stone with the merchant or study more about its healing and esoteric qualities. Using a combination of intuition, knowledge and touch, you will discover the crystals most suitable for you. You can also bring your pendulum with you to the gem shop and use it to read which crystals are most in tune with your personal energy.

On a concluding note, be aware of the shapes, sizes and processes that go into crystals. You will find highly polished stones that make beautiful pendants, but to me, all that polishing and processing distract from the pure, natural aesthetics of the stone.

Thus, I much prefer a raw, unpolished stone just as it was found in the earth.

On the other hand, crystals can be very artistically crafted into wands, spheres or hearts. My experience is that crystals shaped into round balls can be a bit problematic. I discovered this one day during Reiki training when I placed a round purple amethyst on a student's heart. Well, no sooner did they take a deep breath when the crystal went rolling off their chest, onto the floor and proceeded to roll very noisily all away across the room. Get the picture? It was embarrassing to say the least. Since then, I've returned to my "old faithful" naturally shaped amethyst.

## Conclusion

Reiki 2 introduces fascinating and challenging aspects to your personal transformation. Take your time, apply all the techniques and experience all the processes of change that are necessary for you at this time in your life. The changes and healing can hardly be quantified. You are the best judge of your own growth, healing and transformation. For sure, consult with your teacher and friends to reflect on your growth and how to progress further along your path. Ultimately, you will know for yourself.

Your Reiki 2 teacher may certify you immediately upon completion of the training course or may ask you to complete a series of healings and procedures before conferring a certificate of achievement. For my Reiki 2 students to receive certificates, I require that they perform a series of self healings on themselves for every year of their life. I also require them to conduct a variety of distance healings with their family, friends, patients and with me. I suggest that students document their healing experiences. All of these steps support the teacher's dedication to the student's progress. I ask students to demonstrate a similar level of dedication to themselves and to Reiki.

# Chapter Seven

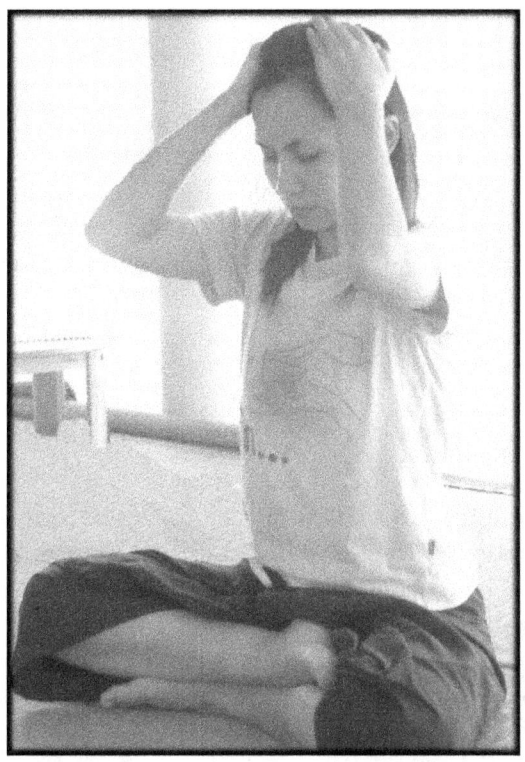

# A Holistic Approach to Personal Transformation

Having studied this far, you have already made significant progress in your understanding of Reiki. Please remember that Reiki is much more than an intellectual pursuit. Just reading this book is only a fraction of the totality of Reiki education. The vast majority of the Reiki experience is visceral and must be accessed with body, mind and spirit. This chapter explores several practices that you may pursue to supplement your long term development. These techniques are woven together from elements of Reiki, Pranayama, Kundalini and Taiji. Parallels and relationships exist between these disciplines, but they are not synonymous. This chapter provides a brief overview and shares basic instruction in a variety of techniques that you can incorporate into your personal transformation regimen. All of these practices can enhance your ability to channel Reiki. To specialise in any of these techniques, seek experienced teachers to guide you further.

The final three chapters in this book explore the interdisciplinary potential of Reiki. The exercises, techniques and concepts described here are equally applicable for all levels of Reiki. I aim to inspire and instruct Reiki practitioners to develop themselves beyond the traditional hand positions, attunements and symbols. Even if you choose not to be trained in Reiki, you will find many valuable ideas in chapters seven, eight and nine that you can immediately apply in your life.

**Pranayama**

The Yogic name for life force is "prana." The flow of prana means the flow of energy. The science of Yogic breathing is known as "Pranayama." The following exercises will help you gain greater control over your breath, deepen your breathing and nurture keener awareness of your breathing process. These techniques are essential for purification of the "nadis" which are the energy channels of the body. In Yogic philosophy, mind and prana are not structurally different from each other. Prana manifests as mind. When mind becomes disturbed, prana also gets disturbed which results in breathing imbalances. Similarly, when prana is unhealthy, mind becomes unhealthy leading to psychological imbalances.

Imbalances in breathing disturb the physiological functions and can become pathological. Diseases such as asthma, hypertension and migraines are the result of such imbalances. Dr. Gabriel Cousens explains that the deeper you breathe, the easier it is to remove excess acid from your system by exhaling carbon dioxide. Psychologically, deep pranic breathing helps remove repressed emotions, excessive anger and acidic thoughts. Knowledge and practice of breathing exercises benefit your overall personal health.

Inhaling brings prana into the body, while exhaling removes old, stale energy from the abdomen called "apana." Deep Yogic breathing begins with expansion of the abdomen followed by expansion of the ribs. As the lungs fill, the chest and shoulders are lifted. The Yogic breath completely expands the lungs in every direction while filling with fresh oxygen and pranic energy. Exhaling in Yogic breathing reverses the process. First, the shoulders lower and the chest contracts to its resting state. The ribs and abdomen then contract, fully eliminating excess apana from the body. In each of the exercises below, please note whether the practice focuses on breathing from the abdomen, the chest, or employs the complete Yogic breath.

As a Reiki practitioner, you can suggest these practices to family, friends and patients who are suffering from weakness, apathy or respiratory illness. The following breathing exercises are derived from the disciplines of Pranayama and Kundalini.

### Activating Breath

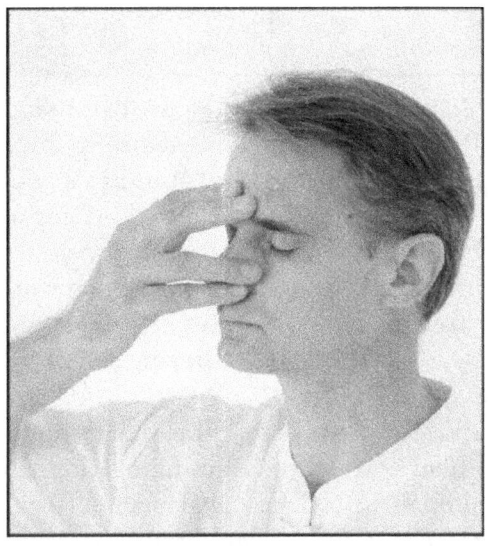

A beginning Pranayama technique is called the activating breath. Activating breath is most suitable for practice in the morning. Raise your right hand placing your index and middle fingers on your brow chakra. Close your left nostril using the fourth and fifth fingers of your right hand as shown in the picture. Breathe in only through the right nostril for 5 seconds and exhale only through the right nostril for 10 seconds. Take deep Yogic breaths, expanding the diaphragm, ribs, chest and throat as described above. Repeat the activating breath 15 to 20 times. Respiration exclusively through the right nostril activates sun energy called "pingala." Practise this technique each morning before, during or after your meditation practice. This will energise you and prepare you for the day.

## Calming Breath

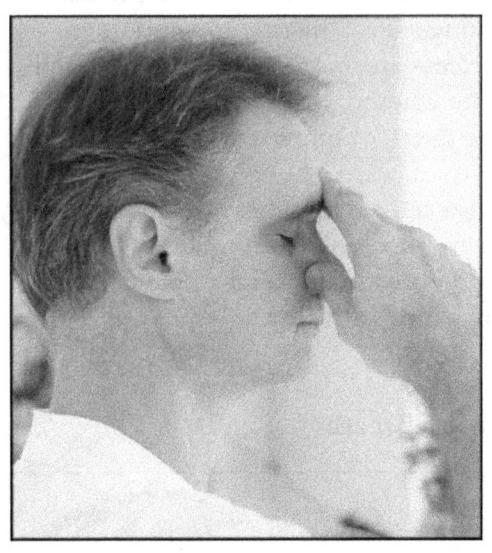

The calming breath is especially suitable in the evening before you go to sleep. To begin, lift your right arm and close your right nostril with your right thumb. Place your right index and middle fingers on your brow chakra as shown in the photo. Inhale exclusively through the left nostril, for a count of 5 seconds. Exhale only through the left nostril for a count of 10 seconds. Breathe deeply taking a full Yogic breath expanding the diaphragm, ribs, chest and throat. Practise the calming breath 15 to 20 times. Respiration exclusively through the left nostril stimulates cooling moon energy called "ida." This technique can be practised during your evening meditation or before going to bed. It will calm your mind and contribute to improved sleep much better than watching the nightly news!

## Alternate Nostril Breathing

Each of these Pranayama breathing techniques has a positive healing effect on the body and mind. Alternate nostril breathing (nadi shodana) produces a balancing effect. It can serve as an effective tool to keep you balanced during the day, especially if you work in a busy office. Use alternate nostril breathing any time you feel stressed or unbalanced. To practise, lift your right arm and close your right nostril with your right thumb. Place your right index and middle fingers on your brow chakra. Breathe in exclusively through the left nostril and then close it using your fourth and fifth fingers. Relax the pressure of your thumb and exhale exclusively out your right nostril. Repeat the process, vice versa, breathing in through the right nostril, out through the left to complete one circuit. Repeat 15 to 20 circuits. Breathe at a normal, natural pace throughout the exercise. Maintain a state of meditation and allow the air to breathe your body.

You can incorporate these three Pranayama techniques into your daily meditation practice or Reiki self healing sessions. Practise the activating, calming and alternate breathing techniques for one to three months, gradually increasing your capacity. This prepares you for more advanced Pranayama and Kundalini techniques. The next breathing practice is substantially more intense.

## Breath of Fire

Kundalini Yoga is concerned with raising the dormant energy coiled in the root chakra. Like Pranayama, the practice of Kundalini involves control of the breath. Using a variety of breathing techniques and physical postures, Kundalini energy is awakened to rise up through all your chakras to your crown. The following technique is called "breath of fire" or "kapalabhati." This is a powerful breathing technique that raises your energy level and body temperature.

Sit in the lotus position and meditate with your hands resting on your knees. Quickly and forcefully pull in and up on your abdominal muscles, pumping all the stale air from the bottom of your lungs out your nose. Immediately relax your muscles and allow your abdomen to expand naturally. Repeat this movement using only the muscles of the diaphragm, pumping the air out of your lungs as rapidly as you can. Air is forcefully expelled from your nostrils in short, brisk bursts. When you relax your abdominal muscles, your diaphragm automatically draws in fresh air as if filling a vacuum.

Breath of fire strengthens the abdomen, activates the second and third chakras, and greatly increases the oxygen and prana available to your brain. It purifies your entire respiratory system. In the beginning, practise kapalabhati 20 times followed by a long, deep breath. Hold it for several moments and then slowly exhale. Relax with a few normal breaths and then resume for 20 more rapid breaths followed by a deep breath and a period of rest. Gradually increase your practice up to three minutes. Do not push yourself too hard. If at any time you feel dizzy, feint or exhausted, simply stop the procedure and resume normal breathing. Rising Kundalini energy destroys the ego, leads to enlightenment and a merging with the universe. It is recommended that you study with an experienced Kundalini instructor if you are interested in practicing intensely.

Breath of fire is most suitable in the mornings and afternoons because of its energising effect. Practise outdoors or in a well ventilated room. Include this technique in your meditation practice, your Reiki self healings or as part of your Yoga routine. Practise any time you are feeling heavy in the head or congested in your respiratory system.

## Inter-Disciplinary Chakra Energising Routine

Yogic science includes a vast array of exercises in addition to the Pranayama and Kundalini techniques described so far. The following section offers a chakra by chakra routine for holistic development. These techniques have been developed from the philosophies and methodologies of several approaches including Vipassana meditation, Pranayama, Kundalini and Taiji.

## The Root Chakra

Your root chakra is located at the base of your spine. This chakra can be exercised using a "bandha," which refers to the locking of a chakra. Locking chakras helps to contain the flow of energy and increase your potential for channelling Reiki. Be careful to practise these techniques gradually, never pushing yourself beyond your limits. Seek the advice of a skilled Yoga teacher for further guidance and more specific explanation of the muscles involved.

To employ "mula bandha," sit in the lotus position and place one of your heels at your perineum, the space between your anus and genitals. Mula bandha is a contraction of the perineum muscles. Pull up on your perineum just like when you are stopping the flow of urination. This movement locks your root chakra and prevents energy from flowing back into the earth. While pulling up on the muscles, imagine drawing energy up from the root chakra and sending it upwards towards your crown.

Mula bandha focuses on contraction of the perineum muscles that control urination. It's easy to confuse mula bandha with a closely related technique called "aswini mudra." Aswini mudra focuses on contraction of the anal muscles, an exercise that is helpful for treating haemorrhoids. To distinguish the two muscles, sit with your heel on your perineum and alternate contractions between your anus and perineum. This will help you distinguish between mula bandha and aswini mudra.

Once you have properly distinguished the perineum muscle, practise contracting it for one minute at a time. Then, relax for a moment and contract it again. Continue practicing mula bandha for 5 to 10 minutes. Throughout your practice, keep your eyes closed and be mindful of your breathing. Observe the flow of energy as you practise. If you aspire to become a Reiki Master, these two exercises will serve you well when conducting Reiki attunements. Mula bandha and aswini mudra are also used in the microcosmic orbit of Taiji explained later in this chapter.

## Navel and Solar Plexus Chakras

The navel chakra is located two centimetres (one inch) below the navel while the solar plexus chakra is located in the middle of the abdomen. These chakras can be exercised by employing "uddiyana bandha." To begin, sit in the lotus position while observing your breath. Inhale a normal breath. As you exhale, pull your abdomen up and in as strongly as you can. This action completely forces all the air out of your lungs. Hold in your abdomen tightly for 10 to 15 seconds and then release. Allow your abdomen to expand naturally without any effort. Take another normal breath. As you exhale, firmly contract your abdomen again.

The muscular movement in uddiyana bandha is identical to breath of fire. The difference is that uddiyana bandha is held much longer and breathing is much slower. Contraction of the abdomen expels stagnant air from the bottom of your lungs. Repeat this process 10 times and then return to your normal breathing. Please practise right now to confirm your understanding and application of this bandha. Now, place your hands on your second and third chakras and give yourself Reiki for several minutes. Observe the feelings and sensations in your abdomen and in your mind.

Has your breathing pattern changed in any way? Regularly practicing uddiyana bandha stimulates your liver and digestion system. It contributes to raising vital energy upwards through your chakras. As you've certainly noticed, it trains you to breathe from your abdomen rather than just your chest. I find that this exercise calms me very much and supports me to practise Vipassana meditation for longer periods of time and with much greater calmness of mind.

**The Heart Chakra**

To exercise the heart region, this Kundalini technique loosens up your spine and ribcage to deepen your breathing. Kneel on a cushion and sit on your heels. Reach your arms up and place your hands on your shoulders. Your fingers should be in front while your thumbs are on the back of your shoulders. Hold your elbows so they are parallel to the floor. Now, inhale as you twist your whole body to the left. Then, twist to the right and exhale. Twist your whole body to loosen your spine. Continue for several minutes inhaling from the left, exhaling to the right. After this exercise, place your hands on your heart chakra and give yourself Reiki for several minutes.

    The benefit of this exercise is twofold. It loosens up the spine while increasing the strength of your lungs. This is a good exercise for limbering up prior to sitting meditation. You can also do this during meditation if your back is feeling stiff. May I take this opportunity to remind you to actually DO these exercises! Just reading about them is, how shall we say, useless. The value is in the actual practice. So please, set down the book and practise each of these techniques and observe how your body and mind respond.

## The Throat Chakra

I would like to offer three exercises for the throat, neck and shoulders to loosen up the region around your throat chakra. The first is a Kundalini technique that we can call shoulder shrugs. Kneel as in the previous exercise or return to the lotus position, whichever you prefer. As you inhale, lift both shoulders up as high as they will go as shown in the photo. When you exhale, drop your shoulders strongly to force the air out of your lungs. Lift your shoulders again as you breathe in, expanding your lungs up into the chest and shoulder region; drop your shoulders quickly and heavily as in a very adamant sigh of relief. Yes, it should be noisy! Exhale forcefully enough that you create a hissing sound from your nose. Not only does this give you carte blanche to make so-called "rude" noises, it also helps expel additional toxins. Continue this exercise for 1 or 2 minutes and then return to normal breathing. This loosens your shoulder and neck muscles allowing your lungs to expand upwards more completely. It can also be performed while you're slaving in front of your computer all day. For those doing repetitive, stationary office work, incorporate shoulder shrugs into your "office Yoga" routine. It's up to you whether or not you employ the hissing sounds at the office!

    The next exercise involves twisting your neck. Sit comfortably in whichever position you prefer. Turn your head all the way to the left while inhaling. Then, turn your head all the way to the right while exhaling strongly through the nose creating a sniffling sound. Continue for 1 minute at a comfortable pace. Then reverse the process: Turn your head to the right while inhaling and then turn to the left while exhaling forcefully through your nose. The speed and amount of force that you employ depend on your strength and flexibility. At first, move slowly and gently. As you warm up and develop a smooth rhythm, increase your pace and the force used to expel air from your lungs.

I remember the first time I taught this technique to a group of Korean teenagers. They couldn't stop laughing because they were mostly concerned that mucus would be ejected from their noses. Indeed, you can expect mucus or congestion to be released during this exercise so you might want to keep a handkerchief at your side. These exercises aim to relax your body, loosen your muscles and deepen the strength of your lungs. In the meantime, you benefit from an increase in oxygen, enhanced prana and improved concentration.

A third exercise for the throat chakra is called "ujjayi Pranayama" which mimics the sound of ocean waves. In this practice, lower your chin while slightly contracting your throat. This creates a snoring or purring sound in your throat. Please note that no noises are made in your nasal passages. Ujjayi breathing focuses specifically on clearing the throat and chest areas. Practise ujjayi Pranayama for several minutes while meditating between exercises.

All of these exercises can be integrated into your Reiki self healing practice. Give yourself Reiki at the throat chakra for several minutes between exercises.

## The Brow Chakra

How can you exercise the brow chakra? It might not seem like your brow and forehead have many muscles, but this exercise will show you otherwise. I call this the eye crunch technique. We teach this technique in our holistic health courses during deep relaxation sessions after lunch (you could call them naps if you like). Sit comfortably and take a deep Yogic breath. When your lungs are full, hold your breath while contracting all your eye muscles as tightly as you can. Squeeze tightly for several moments until you tire; then quickly release all the air from your lungs in a burst. Take a few normal breaths to relax. Repeat up to 10 times.

The next step of the exercise involves clenching the whole face. Take a deep Yogic breath. When your lungs are fully expanded, hold your breath while contracting all your facial muscles as tightly as you can. It feels as if you are making your face smaller. Use every muscle in your forehead, around your eyes, cheeks and jaws. Hold for several moments before releasing with a strong burst of air. Then take a few breaths to allow your breathing to return to normal. Perform this exercise up to 10 times. How do you feel? Are you more aware of the muscles in your face? Did the exercise release tension?

Continue sitting in a meditative posture for 10 minutes after the exercise. Place your hands on your brow chakra and ask Reiki to flow. Notice the quality of your mindfulness and concentration. As with all the exercises and techniques in this chapter, they can be practised individually or as a set, whichever suits you at the time. The eye crunch and face clench are very suitable for "impromptu stress release" whether you are working late at the office or stopped in heavy traffic.

## The Crown Chakra

To exercise your crown chakra, I suggest doing what Yogi Bhajan named "ego eradicator." Sit in the lotus position and raise your arms over your head at 60 degree angles. Keep your chin slightly tucked down towards your chest throughout the exercise. Gently close your four fingers so your fingertips lightly touch the base of your fingers as shown in the photo. Point your thumbs at each other above your head. Close your eyes and focus your attention in the region above your crown chakra where your thumbs are pointing. Begin the breath of fire exercise described earlier. Continue for 2 or 3 minutes until you get tired. Then, bring your thumbs together touching over your head and open the rest of your fingers.

To conclude this practice, sweep your arms around your aura, closing the aura as practised in chapter three. This gesture smoothes out your aura and surrounds you with positive healing energy. This exercise strengthens your lungs and empowers concentration at your highest chakra. Together, these minimise the ego and support you on your path towards universal consciousness.

## Becoming the Breath

A holistic way to round out this series of breathing and physical exercises is what I call becoming the breath. Sitting in meditation, imagine the breath is filling your whole body from your feet up to your head. As you breathe in, imagine air and prana filling your bones and your muscles. Imagine the air is filling all your organs and tissues. As you exhale, imagine old air being released from every part of your body. Breathe in again as you perceive yourself becoming the breath. Then exhale completely, observing the breath dispersing.

In the pause between breaths, recognise the total absence of self. Again, inhale a full body breath as you become the breath. The whole body is breathing in. Become the breath. Exhale fully, recognising the temporary nature of every breath. Become the breath. Recognise the temporary nature of the concept of self. Release the self in the same way that you release the breath.

May I add one very simple, yet very powerful procedure to this technique? Smile. As clichéd as this may sound, smiling is probably the healthiest thing you can do. Smile. Advice to use an inner smile dates back thousands of years to the teachings of Taiji. Smile.

## Taiji

"Taiji" (sometimes spelled "Tai Chi") is concerned with the balance and flow of energy known as "qi" (pronounced as "chee" and sometimes spelled "chi"). Qi refers to both internal and environmental energy. The qi of the universe influences the qi in your body. Taiji is a relaxing and energising system of moving meditation that is timed to the flow of qi in your body which moves about 20 centimetres (8 inches) per second. As you practise, you become more sensitive and aware of body qi. This awareness is helpful during Reiki sessions for reading the flow of energy in your patients.

You can observe Taiji practitioners in the early mornings at local parks in many cities around the world, particularly where many Chinese people are resident. Taiji brings grace to your movements, focus to your mind and keeps you well rooted in every step. Of course, it takes time to learn and requires a lot of practice. You can learn the concepts from a book, but studying the movements requires the patient guidance and wisdom of a Taiji master.

Daoism (sometimes spelled Taoism) is an ancient Chinese philosophy that describes the way to bring your mind, body and the universe into harmony. The Daoist view of life is that human activity should flow gently like a river. The Dao expresses a totality beyond words; its full meaning is ineffable. Like Buddhism, the focus in Daoism is on the here and now. Daoism perceives the movement of qi in terms of energy points, channels and meridians in the body such as those stimulated in acupuncture.

Qi is also observed according to your stage in life, the seasons, the movements of the sun, the moon and the time of day. Indian Yoga and Chinese Taiji overlap in many regards, but they employ different names, concepts and explanations of how energy works. The present section discusses energy in the Daoist sense to complement your Reiki practice. Taiji complements your Reiki practice by increasing awareness of energy and developing the power to direct energy at will.

Daoism stresses the circulation of energy through the energy channels of the body. It is concerned with the balance of "yin" and "yang" energy. Daoist healing energy involves completing two main channels in the body. Earthly yin energy rises through the feet and legs up to the "hui yin" centre located at the perineum between the genitals and anus (correlating to the root chakra). Energy then moves up the spine to the crown from where it descends to the point between the eyes (correlating to the brow chakra). Meanwhile, heavenly yang energy flows from the universe into the crown chakra. These energies flow down the front of the body from the brow to the root chakra. When these circuits are connected, energy is circulated using the microcosmic orbit.

**Microcosmic Orbit**

The microcosmic orbit involves consciously directing energy around the body. Contracting the hui yin increases your ability to draw energy up from the earth and hold it. To do this, pull up on your perineum and rectal muscles together. This position combines mula bandha and aswini mudra described in the root chakra exercise. At first, hold this position for 30 seconds. Practise until you can hold it for 5 to 10 minutes at a time.

The next part of the microcosmic orbit involves using your tongue to link the yin (feminine, cooling) and yang (masculine, warming) energy. Lightly place your tongue on the roof of your mouth, just behind your front teeth to draw energy through your crown into your body. Placing your tongue on your palate completes the energy circuit of yin and yang. Close your eyes and visualise qi energy flowing.

Qi flows from the root chakra, up the back of your spine to your crown chakra. From the crown chakra, qi flows down to the brow, down to the point where your tongue is pressed against the palate of your mouth. From there it flows down the front of your body and passes through all the chakras until it reaches your root chakra. Close your eyes and mentally move the qi through this circuit. Focusing your mind on the flow of energy synchronises mind, body and qi.

This procedure can effectively be used to intensify Reiki (qi) in your body. When you are ready, incorporate this technique into your Reiki healing practice. Combine the micro-cosmic orbit with Reiki very gradually, just a minute or two at a time. With hui yin contracted and your tongue pressed to your palate, direct Reiki to flow out from your palm chakras. Place your hands on your patient and allow the intensified Reiki to flow into them. To study more specific details of how to circulate energy through your body, I recommend "Awaken Healing Energy through the Tao" by Mantak Chia for a complete explanation of Taoist energy. His book explains the collection and grounding of energy for your optimum vitality.

**Summary**

With so many overlapping concepts and techniques presented in this chapter, it may be helpful to include this brief summary of each of the sciences presented here.

The history of Reiki reaches back about 100 years to Dr. Usui, who discovered the symbols, techniques and philosophy of healing during a 21 day fasting meditation. Reiki is the name that he gave to universal energy. This is not to say that the energy itself is only 100 years old. In fact, all energy is as old as the universe. Indeed, the universe is the energy and the energy is the universe.

The art and science of Taiji dates back thousands of years to ancient China and involves physical and conscious movement of internal and environmental qi.

Yoga developed in ancient India thousands of years ago and includes a wide variety of arts and sciences including physical postures known as asana, breathing practices known as Pranayama and the raising of powerful energy that is coiled at the root chakra known as Kundalini. Additionally, Yogic practice involves a wide array of moral, ethical and spiritual guidelines that are effectively explained in "The 8 Limbs of Yoga" by Bhava Ram which is based on Patanjali's Yoga Sutras. For purposes of the present explanation, we can say that prana is essentially the same energy as qi or Reiki.

Please note that these names essentially refer to the same energy, but they are not synonymous.

I've tried to show the relationship between these disciplines and how they can be effectively combined for your optimum development. Decide for yourself if you will strictly adhere to one set of practices or pursue an inter-disciplinary approach.

## Dimensions of Health

What if you found out you or a loved one had cancer? Heart disease? Diabetes? AIDS? High blood pressure? Depression? These are serious questions that at some point in our lives, all of us must answer. As a responsible family member or as a responsible Reiki practitioner, these questions may soon be on your agenda. I would like to elicit your knowledge and awareness of the numerous dimensions of health care issues to help prepare you for responding to any of the above health issues should they arise in your life.

I would like to conclude this chapter with several questions: What is the direction of your continuing development? What do you need to learn more about? What do you need to practise more regularly? To help you address these questions, I'd like to ask what you consider the dimensions of your health. Complete the checklist on the next page and see how holistically you conceptualise health care. Feel free to consider what other dimensions could well be included in your own holistic concept of health.

Many of the ideas in the following chart were generated by participants at an Ecological Design Education (EDE) course at Wongsanit Ashram in Thailand during a session that focused on personal and planetary healing. For each of the categories identified below, evaluate yourself in terms of knowledge, practice and priority in terms of your personal health care programme. Decide which dimensions of health you want to research more thoroughly.

| Dimension of Health | Your Knowledge on a scale of 1 to 10 | Your Development on a scale of 1 to 10 |
|---|---|---|
| Attitudes / emotions | | |
| Breathing / Pranayama | | |
| Buddhist wisdom of suffering and death | | |
| Community (acceptance) | | |
| Dangers of GMO food | | |
| Dangers of dairy products | | |
| Earth (mud) therapy | | |
| Elimination/detoxification | | |
| Exercise | | |
| Fasting (juice or water) | | |
| Herbal Therapy | | |
| Laughter therapy | | |
| Love | | |
| Meaningful work and reasons to live | | |
| Mindfulness | | |
| Nutrition | | |
| Organic food vs. chemical fertilisers | | |
| Pharmaceutical dangers | | |
| Planetary healing | | |
| Psychology | | |
| Reiki, Qi, Prana | | |
| Self Knowledge and self acceptance | | |
| Social Environment | | |
| Sound therapy | | |
| Spiritual practice, religion | | |
| Sun therapy | | |
| Surgery | | |
| Thoughts and beliefs | | |
| Vaccine dangers | | |
| Veganism | | |
| Water therapy | | |
| **Where will you begin?** | | |

# Chapter Eight

# Natural Healing, Healing Nature

Deep personal transformation through Reiki extends far beyond healing individual human beings. The greatest sources of healing come from both within ourselves and from the world around us. We have a responsibility not only to our personal health and transformation, but to the health and evolution of our planet. This chapter embraces Nature for Healing as well as Healing for Nature.

### Naturopathy and Reiki

Can Naturopathy cure diabetes? Can it cure cancer? High blood pressure? We frequently hear these questions from participants in our holistic Reiki health courses. The phrasing of these questions reveals the embedded ideological power of allopathic Western medicine. That is, many people wait for illness and then go to a doctor to seek a cure. This approach is insane! Yet, the vast majority of people wait for illness rather than implementing preventative and empowering health care practices. Further, this ideology motivates the purchase of health insurance as if some large corporation could actually "insure" your good health. The main thing that an insurance company insures is that they make outstanding profits year after year.

Does having insurance make you feel more secure? Is it possible that people neglect their physical health based on the illusion that health insurance protects them? Is purchasing insurance actually an investment in the prophecy that you are going to get sick? Does dependence on insurance for a sense of security undermine your personal empowerment? The practice of Naturopathy circumvents most of these concerns by creating a powerful synergy between you and nature.

Vaccines are another form of so-called insurance against disease. While history shows that some vaccines have heralded amazing health benefits, this does not imply that all vaccines are necessary or safe; quite the contrary. Manufacturers of vaccines are most assuredly seeking record breaking profits in the years to come. Do they have a vested interest in the pandemic spread of disease because that means incredible demand for their drugs? If you have any doubts of the profit motive, research the marketing projections for the next decade of corporations that produce vaccines. Look at the agenda of the World Vaccine Congress where industry leaders discuss how to benefit from the spread of disease. They go so far as referring to "blockbuster vaccines" in their marketing lingo. You'll see they are perched like vultures predicting the next pandemic. This is how the "health-care" industry functions. Naturopathy takes a radically different approach to immunity.

By placing your faith in government and its regulations, insurance companies and their claims adjusters, or vaccine manufacturers and their profit motive, are you abandoning and betraying your personal responsibility for optimising your own health? The only authentic insurance that you can establish for your health is a programme dedicated to nourishment, strong immunity and pro-active practices in every dimension of health. True immunity implies strength and cleanliness of your entire being, not just some trendy chemicals brewed with mercury and jabbed into your butt ostensibly to protect you. Vaccines may assuage your fears and lull you into a false sense of security. They may disempower you from truly managing your own health care programme. More seriously, some vaccines are implicated in the cause of disease rather than the prevention of disease. Naturopathy, like Reiki, aims to empower you to strengthen and heal yourself naturally.

Naturopathy may not be able to cure every disease, but proponents explain most assuredly that it can prevent virtually every disease. Prevention is the main point of Naturopathy. As our Naturopath friend Dr. Ravindra Nisal in Pune, India teaches: Naturopathy is not just a cure, it's a way of life. Naturopathy does not offer a standard remedy for every person. Rather, it offers a programme designed to meet the unique needs of each person at every stage of life. Nature is not standardised any more than people are standardised. Healing with Naturopathy, as with Reiki, needs to be individualised according to person, place and condition of health.

The most insightful concept that I've learned from Naturopathy concerns the great misconception of disease in modern society. What is the misconception? Allopathic Western medical practice generally considers colds, runny noses, flu, coughs, menstruation and diarrhoea as diseases. In fact, these are the body's natural way of cleansing. Sneezing, coughing, sweating and bleeding are all perfectly ordinary measures of detoxification that the body manages by itself. In most cases, these processes operate just fine without external intervention. Belief that these conditions are "diseases" justifies chemical intervention to suppress a cough, stop a runny nose or diarrhoea. This belief deceives virtually everybody that I know.

While certainly there are cases when pharmaceuticals can be very helpful, in many cases they interfere with the body's natural system of cleansing. The trick is to be well enough informed and wise enough to know when to let nature do its duty and when to trust a chemical to assist your healing. When pharmaceutical toxins collect in the body, they contribute to extremely dangerous conditions including liver and kidney failure. Just look at the fine print on the labels or research on the internet and you'll see a dandy list of life threatening conditions that are caused by the ingestion of legally prescribed pharmaceuticals. Nature, on the other hand, poses no dangerous side effects.

In addition to your ordinary system of detoxification, our Naturopath friend Dr. Jacob Vadakkanchery from Kerala, India recommends "extra-ordinary" measures of detoxification. These procedures include using a "neti pot" to rinse the nose and sinuses, eye wash, lemon juice gargle, water enema, fruit fasting and juice fasting. All of these procedures detoxify the body more intensely than the ordinary day to day cleansing routines of the body.

It's somewhat ironic that as I explain more "advanced" techniques of healing and personal transformation, the suggestions become increasingly basic; namely, food, water, inner hygiene and breathing. This is a rather radical approach that penetrates to the very roots of human existence in its most elemental forms. This approach might even seem diametrically opposed to "advances" in modern medicine that include super chemical brews and high-tech laser surgeries.

Dr. Jacob explains that all diseases are caused by the accumulation of morbid and toxic matter in the body. He explains that the root cause of disease is not bacteria as claimed by Western allopathic doctors; rather, bacteria grow after the accumulation of toxic matter, creating a favourable environment for their reproduction. In this perspective, acute diseases represent the body's efforts to cleanse itself and remove the toxins. Therefore, the body should be supported in this natural process and encouraged through extra-ordinary cleansing techniques rather than using drugs to suppress the symptoms. The human body, like all animals, has internal mechanisms for self-healing which are best stimulated by natural means. Food, correctly used, is medicine. Similarly, fasting is a powerful therapy that cleanses the body and lightens the heart at the same time.

### Naturopathy and Fasting

My personal experience with fasting has proven to be one of the most extraordinary experiences that I've had along the path of cleaning up my health and my life. Fasting gives the digestion and elimination systems a much needed rest, allowing the body to remove toxins, dead cells and excess fats more thoroughly. Fasting can be based on seasonal fruits, raw vegetables, limited to the intake of freshly squeezed fruit juices, the juice of fresh coconuts, or in a more intense form by consuming only fresh water. Fasts can range anywhere from 12 hours to 21 days! Fasting for 12 hours implies not eating anything after 6 p.m. until breakfast the next morning. Alternatively, a semi-fast would consist of nibbling on fresh fruit in lieu of your evening meal. This approach provides a light and fresh snack that is easy to digest and allows your digestion system to rest more deeply while you sleep.

Fasts of 1 to 3 days can be conducted on just fruits, just vegetables, or just fresh fruit juices. This type of fast assures sufficient energy and vitamins while greatly simplifying the work load on the stomach and intestines. Fasts of any kind are generally well supported by implementing "news fasts," "computer fasts" and "telephone fasts." That is, give your body and mind a true and complete rest.

Fasting should always be pursued gradually and you should be particularly cautious when breaking a fast. For example, when I conduct a seven day juice fast, it actually requires 10 to 12 days to complete the entire cleansing programme. I pre-fast on fresh fruits for at least 2 days, followed by 7 days on freshly squeezed fruit juices and water, followed by at least 2 days on fresh fruits. After that, I incrementally introduce raw vegetables and cooked vegetables to my diet until my stomach regains full digestive power.

During the fasting period, it may be necessary to employ water enemas to assist the elimination of wastes in the intestines. Break fasts by eating very slowly, chewing very thoroughly and eating very small portions. I find that 7 days fasting on juice is relatively easy, but breaking the fast for the next several days is quite hard for me to handle because it requires even greater self control. Throughout my fasting period, I always give myself at least a full hour of Reiki self healing each day in addition to several meditation sessions. I also do some light Yoga each day in the early morning sun. Avoid heavy or strenuous exercise while fasting.

In the case of diabetes, a fruit based fast would not be advisable; in this case, fresh, raw vegetables are much more suitable to help lower blood sugar levels. If you suffer chronic disease, consult with an experienced Naturopath or Yogi who can recommend the optimum fasting method for your health condition. With experience and knowledge, you can extend your fasts and deepen the intensity by limiting your intake to just fresh coconut juice or simply water. As your body cleanses, your mind will freshen, your organs will re-vitalise and every cell in your body will more effectively shed its wastes.

Ironically, fasting the body nourishes the soul! You'll need to experience this for yourself rather than just taking my word for it. Fasting brings greater clarity and calmness to the mind. It also sets the stage for deeper spiritual progress. A very pure body nurtures a pure and peaceful mind.

Please make a careful distinction between fasting and starving. Fasting is a systematic method of minimising food intake while maximising rest to support the detoxification process. Conversely, starvation is when the body is denied food for so long that it begins to consume its own flesh.

Short, one day fasts on a weekly or monthly basis are highly beneficial and enhance your physical, mental and spiritual well being. As you gain experience and deepen your discipline, longer fasts can be pursued. Fasts lasting longer than 7 days should be supervised by an experienced Naturopath or based on a personal fasting programme individually designed for your body's needs. With practice, you will gain the personal insight and wisdom to know how to conduct fasts for optimum benefits. Read widely on this subject and experiment cautiously with your body to determine how you can best benefit from fasting.

## Naturopathy and Water

Have you ever considered the therapeutic benefits of water? Most people may think water is just for drinking, bathing and swimming. Of course, drinking water is the most important thing, but you can also use water for relieving headaches, backaches, constipation and menstrual pains. The challenge in modern society is that most people expect instant cures for their problems. People with migraines expect a magic pill to take away their pain so they can sit at the computer for ten more hours without a break. Other people suffer from sore backs and want a quick drug to relieve the pain, without regularly taking time to limber up, exercise and oxygenate the spine. In Naturopathy, water is used for hip baths, spinal baths, soaking the head and feet. This may sound too simple to be effective, but water presents a very therapeutic effect without any dangerous side effects.

I would like to offer one technique to relieve headaches that we learned at Nisargopchar Naturopathy Ashram. First, rinse your head with cold water for about 5 minutes while keeping the rest of your body dry. Next, wrap your head with a wet towel. Now, draw yourself a bucket of hot water for soaking your feet. Sit down with your feet in the hot water for 10 to 15 minutes. Close your eyes and follow your breathing to calm your mind. At the same time, give yourself Reiki. This technique cools your head while warming your feet, increasing the circulation of blood that releases headache pain. Of course, it's easier to just take a pill, but have you truly considered the potential side effects of pain killers? What can drugs do to your kidneys long term? Have you ever studied the side effects of pain killers? Do you believe those warnings don't apply to you?

Now, the one time when water is not suitable is the most common time that everybody seems to take it. That is, water should never be consumed during meals. Drink water or juice at least 30 minutes before or 30 to 60 minutes after a meal. This is recommended in both Naturopathy and Traditional Chinese Medicine, but for some reason, the average person never learns this at school. During meals, at most, sip a little water or include soup with your meal. Drinking liquids during meals dilutes the digestive juices making it harder for the stomach to accomplish its work.

Maybe you've watched people who use water to gulp down their food. This practice indicates that they are not chewing their food sufficiently and therefore feel it necessary to drink a full bottle of water at every meal. I usually ask friends with this habit if they have teeth in their stomach that will thoroughly chew the food for them once it lands inside. In many cases, they respond that their grandmothers always used to offer the same advice. This is a good case in point where grandmothers know a lot more about health than we learn in health education programmes at school.

If you believe soft drinks and coffee provide adequate water to hydrate your body, you may as well believe that window shopping constitutes sufficient exercise! Fresh water and freshly squeezed juices are by far the best liquids to satisfy the needs of your body. If you crave something a little stronger, green tea is a healthy, tonic option. As all my friends point out, I'm still an avid coffee lover! To my credit, I've cut down from ten cups a day to one cup a day over the last twenty years. I'm pretty happy with this progress, although I know Dr. Jacob will shake his head when he sees me sipping my afternoon java. More recently, my craving for coffee has faded even further since removing milk from my diet.

### Naturopathy and Air

Everybody breathes all day, but do you ever practise breathing? Fresh air is very therapeutic, especially for those of us trapped in big cities. Please don't think that just because you're in air conditioned or climate controlled rooms all day that your air quality is sufficiently healthy. Air conditioners are known to circulate stale air over and over again, spreading germs and dust throughout your office or home. Breathing artificial air that has been inhaled and exhaled dozens of times without any fresh air input is a good way to pollute your lungs. All of us really need more fresh air. This means spending time in the garden, at the park or outside the big city. Fresh air invigorates your lungs, your heart and nourishes every organ in your body without exception. Practise the Pranayama breathing exercises explained in chapter seven for many ways to enhance the quality and quantity of oxygen in your lungs.

Qigong, Chinese Traditional Medicine and Naturopathy all recommend abdominal breathing to replenish the body's energy. I don't know any schools or universities where this is taught. The overwhelming dominance of pharmaceuticals marketed to address every health condition blinds us to our need for plenty of fresh air to be truly strong and vital. It's no coincidence that observation of the breath is a principal technique in Vipassana meditation. Next time you're feeling depressed, sleepy or sluggish, take a good look at your breathing habits before you reach for a chemical solution to your woes.

You can also bring Reiki into your breathing practice while sitting at your desk, in your meditation room, or preferably outdoors. Close your eyes and breathe in while visualising Cho Ku Rei entering your lungs. On your next breath, visualise Sei He Ki as you inhale, visualising it circulating from your lungs into your heart and bloodstream. On the third breath, visualise Ho Sha Ze Sho Nen entering your body and nourishing every cell of your body with highly energised Reiki. Continue breathing like this for 5 to 10 minutes, as long as you enjoy the visualisation and breathing therapy. This is also a good way to review your study of Reiki 2 symbols.

**Naturopathy and Sunlight**

The sun has received a bad reputation in recent years with the prevalence of skin cancer. Yes, sunshine needs to be taken in moderation at appropriate times, but with that caveat in mind, all people truly need sufficient sunshine. The truth is, solar energy is vital to well being. Taiji recommends facing the morning sun as it rises in the east to absorb the yang energy of the sun. Naturopathy recommends going for a walk or practicing Yoga outdoors in the morning to collect the beneficial rays of the sun before it becomes too intense. At home, we place our water bottles out in the garden to absorb the sunshine for one day before drinking it. In Yoga, one of the best known practices is called "surya namaskar," which translates as sun salutations. Whether you practise Yoga every morning or go for a walk in the early hours of the day, be sure you are getting ample natural sunlight. Artificial light in offices and homes may suffice to light the workplace, but these electronic sources of light do not carry the vital life giving energy of the sun.

Natural light is composed of many colours of different wavelengths including all the colours of the rainbow, which are all the colours of the chakras. This demonstrates the inter-relationship between Naturopathy, Reiki, Yoga and the chakra system. All the colours combine to make nourishing white light.

Despite nearly constant propaganda on television and billboards to whiten, lighten and brighten your skin using cosmetics, have you ever seen advertisements to enjoy the benefits of the early morning sun? In fact, sunlight is anti-bacterial, anti-inflammatory and anti-allergenic. Anybody in Scandinavia can attest that sunlight is an effective anti-depressant. With all these properties, let's hope that nobody tries to monopolise the market on sunlight because it truly is the greatest power in our part of the universe.

Sorry, this doesn't give you a license to sunbathe all day long. Rather, strive to benefit from the natural, free bounty of solar energy early in the morning or late in the afternoon. If you are cycling across the country during the summer, by all means, take appropriate precautions to protect your skin from the dangerous effects of intense and prolonged exposure to mid-day sun.

# Naturopathy and Earth

Despite the fact that humans live on Earth, many of us are grossly divorced from it. I always used to ask my poetry students at Srinakharinwirot University when the last time was they actually touched the earth, meaning, touched grass, soil or sand with their bare hands and feet. Most of them were stumped and unable to remember the last time they had made direct, physical contact with our planet. Think about it.

We go through our days wearing rubber and leather shoes, walking on concrete, tiles, pavement or travelling in cars, buses and trains. Then, people spend evenings and weekends watching television for how many hours a day? How many hours in a month? How many hours in a year sitting in front of a box that projects artificial light and artificial truth as well?

Ironically, many people claim that they love to watch so-called nature documentaries on television without recognising how grossly unnatural it is to sit in a climate controlled room watching a box with photos and sounds 1000 hours or more every year. Only on holidays do most people actually take time to walk the beach or picnic in the park. This alienation from earth leaves people very disconnected from the source of life.

Most ancient cultures have developed elaborate ceremonies to honour and respect mother earth, also known as Patchamama in the Inkan tradition in Perú, Bolivia and Argentina. Modern "culture" distracts us from the true culture beneath our very feet. Please, take off your shoes and walk in the garden, stretch out in the park, jog along the beach or do whatever you can to stimulate your relationship with the only planet you can call home. See how this makes you feel. Do you feel better after walking on the grass? Do you feel more grounded? Do your feet feel cooler and more relaxed? I remember when I suggested this technique to my brother John to help him feel more grounded. His response was that there was a foot of snow on the ground and no way was he going for a barefoot walk in the park. Fair enough! So, adjust accordingly!

The sad thing is, most people in modern society have no time for these supposedly "trivial" rituals of getting in touch with our planet. Truth is, getting in touch with your planet will help you get in touch with your self. I trust you will take the time to nurture your relationship with this planet. I trust you will tread gently on this soil.

An additional exercise recommended by Bisong Guo and Andrew Powell in "Listen to your Body" is to put on some old clothes, lie down and roll on the grass to absorb the yin energy of the morning dew. This is a fun way to get all dirty while benefitting from the natural energy of the morning earth. Rolling on the morning dew might seem a little bit crude to those with higher education and a belief that anything wet or dirty should never be touched. This morning ritual can serve as a symbolic gesture of intimacy with the very earth that nourishes and sustains every step of our lives. This is exactly what we need to reconcile this nasty divorce from the earth that so many of us have suffered. This can inspire a reciprocal concern for the well being of our planet for which we are all responsible.

## Naturopathy and Food

You've heard people say, "food is the best medicine." Is this just traditional wisdom, or is it the authentic truth of life on earth? Have you ever heard it spoken that so-called "food" is our most dangerous poison? Industrial food with all its sugars, salts, high fructose corn syrups, colours and preservatives hardly qualifies as food in any genuine sense. Nutrition is an essential aspect of well being. In most cases, it's the primary factor in determining the course of health or sickness. How much fresh, organic food do you eat each day, compared to how much dead and denuded stuff you put in your mouth? How much knowledge do you actually have concerning the energy, enzymes and living qualities of food? Some Reiki students are very eager to learn more and more symbols and healing techniques, yet they refuse to improve their nutritional habits. How can they truly develop themselves with such a narrow approach to healing?

I hate to be the one to bring this up, but most of the lessons we learned at school concerning food are hopelessly outdated and in many cases are contrary to wise nutritional advice. The following section on Veganism offers a brief introduction to the subject. I ask healers to consider these recommendations and support Reiki to be a truly holistic healing discipline.

## Veganism and Reiki

Our Reiki courses always include pure Vegan meals. Vegan food is much cleaner, contains fewer chemicals and is more compatible with the human digestion system than animal products. At the same time, a Vegan life style expresses greater compassion for all living things, is less demanding on the earth's resources and contributes to a more highly sustainable society. Veganism is a profound and effective way to heal nature itself.

As a Reiki healer, it's important to practise compassion and loving kindness towards all beings, including yourself, family and friends, patients and animals. Reiki heals not only at the energetic level, but also provides the healer and patient with information that supports the holistic healing experience. Healing includes making suggestions for improving life style such as exercise and nutrition. It's essential to look more deeply into the health issues that arise with meat based diets compared to Veganism. Many Reiki Masters and healers continue to eat meat. That does not imply that eating meat is healthy at all. It's essential to consider your own dietary patterns and determine your optimum nutritional path.

If someone receives Reiki for their digestion problems but continues to eat frequent servings of meat, then the healing process will be severely limited. To optimise your experience as a Reiki healer or as a recipient of Reiki energy, it's highly recommended to move towards a vegetable oriented diet. A shift towards Veganism can be a gradual transition towards improved health and greater compassion. The pace at which you make these changes depends on how well you are feeling with the changes and the strength of your commitment to change.

What are the benefits of Veganism? A meat-based diet brings numerous issues and controversies onto your plate, including the use of growth hormones to make animals grow faster, antibiotics to prevent or treat disease among animals held in captivity, the violence of slaughter, ethical concerns of eating other living beings, inhumane treatment of animals such as crowded conditions, living in filth, cutting off baby chick's beaks, the toll that a meat culture places on the environment, unsustainable consumption of water, feed and land in addition to the health challenges presented to the human body in digesting meat products and assimilating the chemical brews that make animals grow quickly and cheaply while keeping meat looking pretty and preserving it until it lands on your grill.

## Hormones and Pesticides in your Diet

Sorry, let me slow down a little bit so you can chew on this subject one point at a time. To make animals gain weight more quickly, growth hormones are mixed in with their food. According to various sources, hormones are used in 80 to 90 percent of cattle, pigs and poultry raised in the United States. The National Toxicology programme at the National Institute of Health shows that the estradiol and progesterone used in raising livestock are linked with breast cancer, prostate cancer and the growth of tumours.

Meat eaters have more colon cancer, breast cancer, prostate cancer and ten times more lung cancer than Vegans. A little bit too often, the response that I hear to these details is a paltry, "I like meat." What exactly is in all that meat on your plate? In "Conscious Eating," Dr. Gabriel Cousens describes how farm animals are fed a steady diet of pesticides, hormones, growth stimulants, insecticides, tranquilisers, radioactive isotopes, herbicides, antibiotics, a variety of other drugs and colourants. Is that enough to make you think twice? What is the significance of all these chemicals in your diet?

In 1999, Swiss inspectors detected diethylstilbestrol (DES), the cancer-causing, anti-miscarriage drug, in two shipments of American beef. Keep in mind that this chemical had been banned by the Food and Drug Administration of the United States for growth promotion in chicken and lambs way back in 1959 and totally banned for use in all animal feed in 1979. Is this to suggest that some meat producers are still using illegal chemicals? Is your government truly able to monitor and control the production of meat to safe standards? More recently, the use of growth hormones was banned in Europe. The European Union Scientific Committee states that these hormones pose a risk of cancer, particularly to children. Somewhat predictably, the US cattle industry claims that it produces safe and wholesome beef.

What can we do about these dangers when many people still like to argue that meat is part of their culture? Yes, it's part of some cultures like the Eskimos in northern Canada and the Masai people of Kenya because virtually no other food is available other than meat. In Western culture, students are fed beliefs about the need for meat and protein in school books and relatively few people challenge that information when they mature. Yes, some cultures include a lot of meat in their diet, but does that equate with having a healthy diet?

In "Diet for a New America," John Robbins explains that 95 to 99 percent of all toxic chemical residues in the typical diet come from meat, fish, dairy and eggs. People are correct when they argue that fruits and vegetables also have pesticides and use fertilisers. This is true, but the proportion is relatively tiny compared to the toxins in meat and animal products. Meat has approximately <u>fourteen times</u> more pesticides than vegetables. Ideally, we should all eat organic fruits, vegetables and grains to eliminate all the chemicals from our diets. You would think that governments around the world would be checking and stopping these toxic problems and protecting the people... but governments are often very busy taxing the people and starting wars, leaving little time for protecting our food supply.

## The Production of Meat

Dr. Virginia Livingston-Wheeler explains in "The Conquest of Cancer" that the potential for chickens to have cancer is nearly 100 percent. This is not exactly a good gamble next time you're nibbling on a deep fried chicken wing. Do the animals that you eat have cancer? Would you still eat them if you found out how sick they were when they were slaughtered? Institutes around the world are spending millions of dollars searching for the cure to cancer. This is admirable, but it doesn't seem like anybody is looking at the very dinner plate in front of them for the obvious cause of many cancers afflicting society today.

To maximise profit, industrial food factories crowd animals together in stuffy cages with little fresh air and sunshine. Living under such crowded conditions causes intense stress as well as the potential for rampant disease. It's a very sad irony that the foregoing description sounds uncomfortably similar to the working conditions of your average office worker labouring so hard every day just to earn enough money to pay for insurance, medical bills and taxes.

Animals are routinely fed antibiotics by the ton to minimise economic losses due to disease. Keep in mind that the drugs are used to treat all animals, not only those that are sick. Antibiotics are used to protect the livestock corporation's investment by keeping the animals alive long enough to get them to slaughter. What happens to those chemicals once they are ingested by cows, pigs or chickens? Do these hormones affect the people who eat those dead animals? Which diseases are linked to consumption of these chemicals? An even scarier scenario is that a great deal of bacteria has now become drug resistant because of the overuse of antibiotics in factory farmed animals. The massive use of antibiotics and chemical fertilisers also winds up in our water supply.

Microorganisms that have developed resistance to all antibiotics can lead to epidemic disease in humans and animals. How many global scares have we had in the last ten years concerning pigs, poultry and cows? I'm curious how much profit is generated by the manufacture and sale of vaccines to fight those diseases. Is this enough to make you suspicious if maybe something is wrong with eating meat generously spiced with antibiotics? Would you like go one step further into a process that is largely hidden from the public eye?

## Animal Slaughter

Even if all animal products were indeed clean, safe and free from chemicals, the animals must still be slaughtered to bring them to market. Is that something you could do yourself? Could you bring a knife to the throat of a cow or pig? Would you commit this murder in front of a seven year old child? Could you chop off the head of a scampering chicken or turkey? Have you ever seen this happen in real life or seen it on video? Do you even want to see such violence? Do humans even have a right to do this to animals? Do humans have a responsibility to the earth and other living beings to be humane, ethical and respectful of life? I cannot answer these questions for anybody. All I can do is ask you to ask yourself.

Yes, let me be the first one to tell you that if you ate any chicken or beef today, somebody, somewhere, had to kill that animal to bring it to your plate. Are you, the consumer, therefore culpable for that death? How humanely are the animals slaughtered? Are they gently given a shot to let them peacefully go to sleep, or are they hung up mercilessly from the rafters of the factory? Are their throats slit and their blood allowed to drain all over the floor while they are still alive? Do you know the source and conditions of the slaughterhouse where your meat is processed? Many people say they enjoy a good steak; what if they used different language and said, "I like to eat dead cow." It doesn't sound quite as appetising when we call it what it is.

If this isn't enough, the animals are butchered, cancerous parts included, and the meat is dyed to keep it looking fresh, covered with preservatives to facilitate transport and appear fresh and tasty in your local market. What happens to the preservatives and colourings that are put in every meal? Like all of the other hormones, antibiotics and chemicals, the preservatives and colourings are a substantial part of your diet. All of these concerns directly impact your personal health and the health of those you love. I hope you are beginning to understand why it is incumbent on us to evaluate all these unpleasant points in a book that focuses on personal development.

## Digestion and your Health

What about digesting meat? I eat it every day and have no problems. This may be true for certain people, especially when they are younger, but let's delve more deeply into your digestive tract. Do you have the necessary digestive juices to digest and assimilate beef? Pork? Chicken? Fish? Milk? Eggs? Maybe you can handle some of these animal products, at a dietary level, but have you seriously questioned the mainstream culture of eating meat? Is obesity a concern in your society? Is colon cancer on the rise? Is the consumption of meat implicated in these health issues?

Look at all factors that relate to the gathering, collecting, eating, digesting and elimination of food to gain more comprehensive insight into the nature of our creaturehood. Consider the shape of the human teeth, the length of the human intestines and the time it takes to digest meat compared to a bona fide meat eater such as the tiger. Is your human digestion and elimination system more closely related to meat eating tigers and lions or more closely affiliated with herbivores such as horses? Do your teeth more resemble carnivorous cats and dogs, or more resemble the herbivorous cow? Look at your fingers and consider whether your hands and nails show any resemblance to a leopard's claws or an eagle's talons.

What do these physical attributes suggest concerning the nature of the human being? I'll admit that I did not major in zoology at university, but these questions come to mind when I sit down at the dinner table. I cannot claim that I have deduced the true culinary nature of human beings by analysing their fingers and intestines. I don't claim any teleological proof that humans are biologically designed to live on fruits and vegetables. I only want to pose the questions.

Is your body truly designed to digest the quantity and quality of meat that you consume? Does anybody on television or in the mass media ever raise these questions? The questions are thought provoking, but somehow, they are not part of our educational or cultural discourse. Few of these topics are on the national agenda; they rarely seem to make it into television sit-coms, soap operas or the nightly news. Maybe this is because football games and "reality" shows are so readily available to the public. Reality?

### Veganism and Personal Health

Whatever your political and social position concerning meat-based diets, you still need to think about your personal health. A Reiki healer needs to be healthy and strong in order to heal effectively and serve as a positive role model on the path towards optimum health. The nutritional advantages of Veganism substantially contribute to physical well being. One of the leading causes of death and the major factor that shortens people's life expectancy is heart disease. Heart disease is usually attributed to clogged arteries, hardening of the arteries and increased blood pressure.

Vegans, especially those who consume primarily whole foods, have much healthier arteries by avoiding the bad fats derived from a meat-based diet. This is important for you as a healer, as well as for making sound nutritional suggestions for your patients who come to you with health issues such as high blood pressure, diabetes, poor digestion, constipation, obesity and skin problems. Although you may not be an MD, you are still in a position to guide your patients to make wise nutritional choices.

A great deal of research and evidence indicate the nutritional, environmental and health benefits of Veganism. Life expectancy and quality of health are linked to three important factors that are nurtured by a plant-based diet, namely, fewer bad fats, more anti-oxidants and lower weight. A healthy Vegan diet helps maintain or lose weight, which is linked to longer life expectancy. Still, many people tell me, "I don't like vegetables. I can't get full on vegetables." Well, like veggies or not, people who eat lots of vegetables benefit from intake of many anti-oxidants. Anti-oxidants help your body repair some of the damage caused by aging. The plants you eat provide the raw materials that your body needs to make these repairs.

How many times have people argued: I need my protein! Nutritionist Paavo Airolo states that it's practically impossible to not get enough protein as long as you eat natural, unrefined foods. Of course, nearly everybody that I meet still asks, "How do you get enough protein?" One, adults don't really need that much protein, but at the same time, I get plenty from sunflower and pumpkin seeds, soybeans, leafy greens and fresh fruits. Most people may not realise the scary truth that overconsumption of animal protein contributes to the development of numerous diseases such as arthritis, atherosclerosis, heart disease, cancer and kidney disease. I've read that 26 percent of meat eaters suffer hypertension compared to 2 percent of Vegans. Yes, those are just statistics, so, what is the truth? Everybody needs to make an informed choice.

I would like to bring all of this nutritional information into the practice of Reiki. Many patients who come for Reiki are in need of advice and guidance concerning life style issues such as exercise and nutrition. For example, the first time I met Patricia, she reported serious constipation troubles. She reported having bowel movements only once every four or five days. She didn't realise the seriousness of this condition. Her medical doctors didn't pay any attention to this condition. While Reiki helped her relax, I also recognised her need to take more stringent measures to improve her health. I recommended taking several small steps to improve her digestion and elimination. I suggested that she decrease intake of beef and pork at evening meals while increasing consumption of fibre in the form of vegetables and fruit. I made the suggestions as gradual as possible, hoping that small steps would not meet much resistance. I suggested that she decrease her intake of chicken at evening meals and replace it with vegetables, mushrooms and whole grains. Of course, I can't make these changes for her or for anybody else. Only you can take these steps for yourself. Only you can make the decisions that affect your life. It would certainly be beneficial to research the dangers of meat consumption for yourself.

---

Ajarn Tom,

I always felt that one day I would become a Vegetarian but never thought this soon. I have to thank Reiki and you because it's something I didn't really plan to do quite yet but it occurred on its own as if on purpose but not forcibly. Just yesterday, I decided to eat my favourite pork dish; it turned out I didn't enjoy it that much anymore. By the way, it would be great if you could recommend good veg places around town :) thank you so much!

Donna

---

## The Vegan Transition

Every Vegan has a personal prescription for making a gradual transition to a plant-based diet. Similarly, everyone will have a variety of reasons and motivations for becoming Vegan. I would like to offer a few suggestions for those pursuing optimum health. Minimise or entirely eliminate beef, pork and chicken from your diet. Decrease or eliminate intake of seafood, milk and dairy products. Meanwhile, maximise consumption of fresh fruits and vegetables and experiment with options such as seaweed, seeds and tofu. Experiment with new recipes such as hummus, falafel and other ethnic recipes.

It would also be wise to research the facts and fictions concerning protein, milk, vitamins and supplements. A lot of propaganda has been produced to convince people of the need for milk, vitamins and protein supplements. Rampant marketing has successfully turned nearly every person in society into a customer by convincing them of the need for these products. Careful nutritional planning makes vitamin supplements virtually obsolete.

Every stage of the transition from omnivore to herbivore brings changes to your energy level, detoxification process, digestion and elimination systems. Monitor your own eating and elimination processes as you fine tune the diet that brings you optimum energy and radiance. Each step of the process increases your internal cleansing process, which in turn complements your Reiki growth process.

## Veganism and Spiritual Practice

How does Veganism concern Reiki? Aren't you adding a lot of unrelated topics to your explanation of Reiki? The original Reiki teachings and texts do not comment on the issue of eating animals. From the perspective of personal transformation through Reiki that I advocate, industrial animal farming, slaughter and chemical toxins in meat are all very negative factors in the pursuit of a healthy body, mind and spirit.

Eating dead pigs or chickens seems to be a clear violation of the fifth Reiki Principle: Today, I will be kind to my neighbours and every living thing. Similarly, eating the corpse of a cow seems to be a clear violation of the Sixth Commandment: Thou Shalt not Kill. The First Precept of Buddhism is to abstain from harming or killing living beings. I don't mean to be a perfectionist about this, but I would like to suggest that each person review the principles, commandments and precepts by which they claim to live their lives, and seriously evaluate their adherence to their own principles.

Of course, people still claim that they have free choice to eat meat, fish or eggs. To make that choice ethically, wisely and humanely, please be sure to check the wisdom, humanity, nutritional and health related risks of all factors. You need to know your body's true needs, sift through your cultural beliefs and ideologies and do what is best for your overall health and well being.

In a broader context, have you considered the spiritual aspects of eating meat compared to Veganism? While this may be a very personal matter with a wide variety of responses, it should certainly be addressed. Deep in your heart, how do you feel about the living conditions of farm animals? Do you have a pet cat or dog? What do you think about slaughterhouse conditions? What is your position on animal cruelty? Would you be upset if somebody came in your house and kicked your dog or tried to break the neck of your little sister's pet rabbit? Do animals have souls? Do humans have a right to kill and eat other species?

Visit the "People for the Ethical Treatment of Animals" website to learn more about Vegan ethics, lifestyle and several videos about the suffering of animals. Please don't get me wrong: I don't mean that Vegans are more spiritual and meat-eaters are all heathens! I would just like everybody to consider all dimensions of this issue.

# Veganism and Planetary Healing

Beyond the personal dimension, we all have a responsibility for the health of our planet. Do you consider yourself an environmentalist? Raising a kilogram of beef requires sixteen times the amount of resources as it does to grow a kilogram of vegetables. How many virgin rainforests have been deforested in the interests of raising cattle? How much water is used to raise one cow or one pig? How much feed is required to fatten one chicken or cow? How much pesticide and insecticide is sprayed on the animal feed to keep away pests and how much chemical fertiliser is poured on the crops to maximise the growth of the corn fields? How much of this pesticide, insecticide and fertiliser will end up in your fried chicken dinner tonight? If you're like most people, you may have a very limited comprehension of the severity of these issues.

Dr. Gabriel Cousens writes, "a Vegan diet brings one into ecological harmony with all of creation." It conserves land, water and energy and enhances the quality of life for humans and animals alike. To me, these are important reasons to take further steps in pursuing a Vegan diet. It heals me, saves the lives of animals and helps minimise my impact on the planet. I just consider it being personally and ecologically responsible.

The Food and Agricultural Organisation (FAO) of the United Nations writes that the production of meat and animal products for mass consumption, especially through factory farming, is environmentally unsustainable. Their research shows that the livestock industry is one of the largest contributors to environmental degradation all over the world. Furthermore, modern practices of raising animals for food contribute on a colossal scale to air and water pollution, land degradation, climate change and loss of biodiversity. The FAO initiative concludes that "the livestock sector is one of the most significant contributors to the most serious environmental problems."

> **The Quality of your Soul**
>
> "Is there some inner secret of being Vegan?" Let me share one secret: Once you become a Vegan, your entire life will flourish. Your heart becomes deeper than the society around you. Your mind becomes wider and more profound than you can presently imagine. Becoming Vegan transforms your life at the cellular and spiritual levels. This nourishes your soul to mature and experience wisdom through personal behaviour and experience of a purified body-mind-spirit. This is the inner secret of being Vegan. It's much more than just the food you eat; Vegan nurtures the very quality of the soul.

## Conclusion

I urge you to seek additional ways to minimise all aspects of violence from your life. After ten years as a Vegetarian, I felt a new awareness developing from within myself. After an additional five years as a Vegan, my awareness and compassion have grown exponentially. I realise that when I harbour negative feelings towards anyone, this ultimately leads towards self-inflicted illness. I've learned to recognise that negative, judgmental thoughts are a subtle form of violence. This awareness seems to be the natural evolution of ahimsa, total non-violence within my mind. I work mindfully to diffuse negative feelings and thoughts as they arise.

Please don't mistake me for trying to be a saint or anything like that. Indeed, I still get angry at my neighbours, still get upset when my computer crashes and worry over the state of the world. I don't mean that I've squashed all negativity and now sit on the high throne. I only mean to suggest that through mindfulness and practicing non-violence, I'm able to release a lot of negativity from my life.

Progressing from nutritional aspects of health and spirituality, the final chapter in this book explores transcendent dimensions of being through transformation of the ego, our communities and our planet.

# Chapter Nine

# Planetary Transformation

This chapter extends the exploration of a planetary healing perspective. It takes you beyond self into relationships, social attitudes, community, planetary responsibilities and finally to universal meditation.

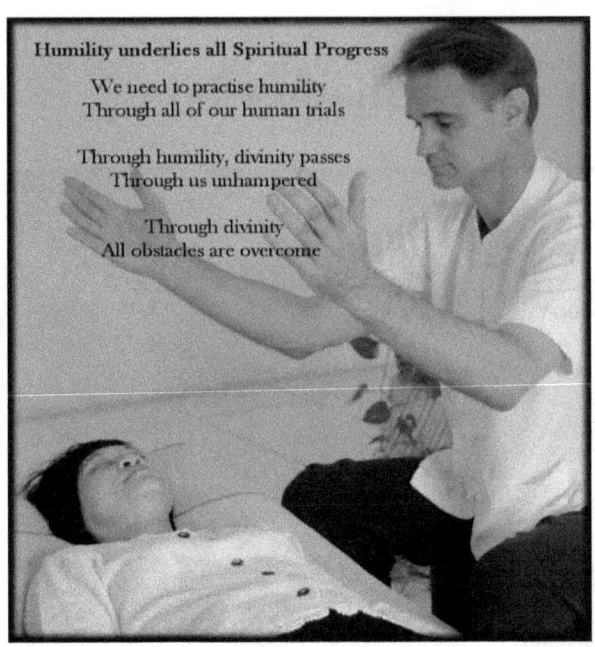

## Beyond Self

Each time I observe myself expressing strong opinions, I ask myself, "does this nurture my humility or propagate my ego?" Guess what? In most cases, my ego is gaining advantage while humility takes a rain check. The ego gets a lot of bad press because it's frequently out of control. As David Hawkins writes in "The Eye of the I," "the self becomes glamorised as the hero of one's life story... the principal actor in the melodrama of life. This requires that the self be defended... and that its survival becomes all important. This includes the necessity to be 'right' at any expense."

When using Reiki, it's helpful to reflect on these thoughts and release the notion that you are the healer and you have the power. It's more effective and truthful to allow the universe to do the healing. Keep in mind, there's no you, no me, just Reiki flowing to bring balance and health. By healing from this perspective, the ego gradually takes a back seat and allows the universe to work its wonders.

Hawkins goes on to say "...one is the witness of phenomena, not the cause... The ego interposes itself between reality and the mind. What we experience in ordinary life is an instant replay of what the ego has just recorded and edited in accordance with its previous programming." This suggests the deeper importance of recognising the ego's persistence in controlling the world and claiming credit for everything. While healing with Reiki, keep your mind as neutral as possible. When wayward thoughts arise, take note and let them go. Return your attention to giving Reiki to your patient. Thoughts left unchecked are a distraction from neutral, impersonal mindfulness.

A transpersonal perspective refers to a dimension of human consciousness beyond normal awareness. It includes expansion beyond personal pleasure and pain. It allows you to see yourself as a spiritual being having temporary human experience. It can transform your dilemmas and permit a wider dimension of healing. Use this approach first with yourself and then you can share it with your Reiki patients. Develop a transpersonal perspective to transcend your ego by practicing the following steps.

- Identify a situation that worries you
- Recognise your beliefs about the situation
- Consider the situation through the eyes of someone who disagrees with you
- Observe the differences in perspective and belief
- Meditate and see the whole situation from a higher perspective
- Visualise someone you highly respect such as Buddha or Jesus handling the situation
- Reflect on the new perspectives and apply them to your situation

Thich Nhat Hanh writes in "Being Peace" that "understanding means to throw away your knowledge." Knowledge, like it or not, blocks the way of understanding. You can enhance your flow of understanding by releasing your knowledge and opinions in order to transcend. This is tricky, especially since our lives seem to consist of nothing more than opinions and knowledge. Ultimately, just be in the moment of who you are with total mindfulness of the moment, completely going with the flow.

Hanh writes further, "Do not think that the knowledge you presently possess is changeless, absolute truth. Learn and practise non-attachment from views in order to be open to receive other's viewpoints." I've found that my greatest barrier to true listening is my open mouth! The open mouth is a like a giant drain that prevents ideas and perspectives from entering the ears and truly absorbing into our minds.

On that note, if your mouth is open too much, maybe it's time to go and eat some fresh fruit or vegetables! Eating healthy food is every bit as important to spiritual development as meditation and taming the ego. As multi-dimensional beings, we need to address every facet of our existence. So, after a particularly enlightening meditation session, secure your spirit in your body and keep yourself well grounded in your earthly guise. As much as we may seek enlightenment, remember to attend to your physical needs with equal mindfulness.

## Transforming yourself through Relationships

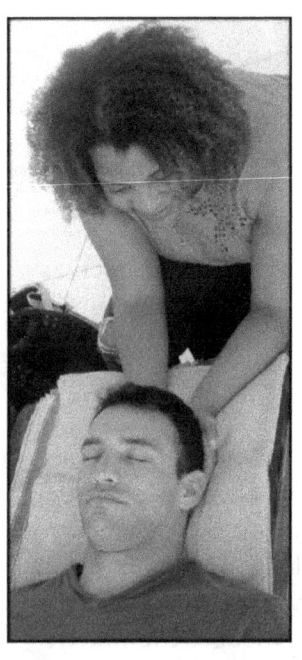

Most of the concepts discussed so far have concerned your inner world. Meanwhile, personal relationships are also a vital part of your healing and growth process. Friends, family and co-workers are the closest people to us. They often serve as our most scrutinous mirrors by which to reflect on self. In their eyes, we can glean honest reflections of who we truly are. Similarly, our thoughts and feelings towards other people incisively indicate how we feel about ourselves and our role in the world. It's very important to exercise mindfulness in our personal relationships for the benefit of all parties involved.

I suggest using the following questions to help you see yourself. Each time you engage in conversation or activity with others and your mindfulness registers negative thoughts, seize the opportunity to transform your criticism into a personal mirror. Whether you're debating with your brother, arguing with your partner or complaining to a shopkeeper, incorporate these questions into your personal search for truth:

1. What is the lesson inherent in this situation?
2. What personal biases have I carried into this situation?
3. Do I seek weaker people in order to make myself feel stronger?

4. Do I identify flaws in other people to distract them from seeing my own weaknesses?
5. Which aspects of my relations are authentic and which are superficial?

As you may recall from chapter two, one of the principles of Reiki involves working, thinking and speaking with honesty. Asking these questions mindfully and reflecting on your response will deepen your personal understanding. These questions are designed to nurture your personal truth and facilitate the healing of your deepest mind. Pausing in mid-debate or mid-argument to ask yourself these questions serves as a powerful wake up call and helps you penetrate the nature of your automatic thoughts.

As you transform your personal relationships, you can apply this ability in healing situations. Very frequently, couples come for Reiki sessions together and invariably they have relationship issues that they hope to resolve through Reiki. By remaining neutral and supportive while asking insightful questions, a Reiki healer can guide both partners to heal themselves and consequently nurture a more positive relationship between them. In addition to individual healing sessions, visualise the Sei He Ki symbol floating between them to ease the tensions in their relationship.

## Transformation of Social Attitudes

Engaging society on a day to day basis is fertile ground for personal transformation. Every situation is a potential healing opportunity. The trick is to be mindful and compassionate as you develop yourself. The meditation and Reiki practices discussed in this book have been designed to support your personal transformation. Now proceed a step further, recognising that every relationship is cause for celebration; every social situation is a magnificent opportunity to pierce your illusions on the path towards ultimate wisdom.

A few sample questions are offered here to support you to realise that your perception of society is a reverberation of your deeper self. From here, create your own challenging questions and answer them for yourself.

1. What do my social opinions indicate about my spiritual development?
2. What do my geo-political views reveal about my mental and emotional health?
3. Is my career conducive to my emotional/spiritual growth?
4. Are the beliefs/products that I promote in my work consistent with my highest values?

**Written Meditation**

Although most of the meditation techniques recommended in this book focus on non-discursive mental silence, this section engages your intellect to analyze situations. A writing journal is a very effective way to explore topics with honest reflection. Call this written meditation.

Written meditation enhances total mindfulness of body, thought, emotion and dharma. This requires heedful intellect rather than allowing your big bossy ego to dictate its dogma. Writing in your personal journal allows you to elaborate your situation succinctly and mindfully at your own pace.

"How can I write if my eyes are closed?" Sit silently at your desk, close your eyes and observe your breath. Calm your mind and relax your body. When you are ready, open your eyes while maintaining continual awareness of your breath. Write down your questions as suggested in the sections above and remain silently in meditation. Keep your mind quiet and allow your deepest intuition to emerge. Open your eyes during meditation long enough to write down your thoughts, then close your eyes and continue to silently observe your mind. Write down answers and solutions as they arise.

Written meditation can complement your silent meditation to focus your energy on resolving pressing issues. Always return to the silence so deeper wisdom can radiate through you without being clogged up by analysis.

Long term, a journal of personal transformation provides a reliable record of the mountains and valleys you have explored in the landscape of your soul.

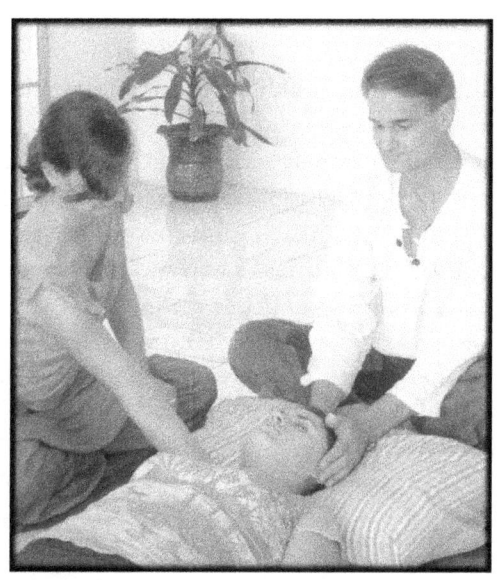

## Healing Community

It's important to establish a community of friends who are healing and developing together. Group meditation is a very powerful practice with your community. When I first started teaching Reiki, our meditations were very brief. Now, we spend 45 to 60 minutes in meditation together. When a diverse group of Reiki students come to our school for training or to join Reiki shares, I lead a community meditation session to benefit each participant and unify the group energy.

A healing community is when the whole group sends loving kindness to one member of the group at a time. Every participant sends Reiki universal energy, friendship and loving kindness for that person's well being. Spend several minutes sending healing energy to each person. Afterwards, discuss each person's experience of the group energy. One student described how she felt waves of energy and peace emanating from all directions of the healing circle. With this in mind, consider seeking the synergy and mutual support provided by group meditation.

Community meditation begins with sending loving kindness, Reiki and compassion to every member of the group. Once all participants are in deep meditation, the group collectively radiates loving kindness outwards. Radiate compassion to your families, neighbours, then to your district, radiating further to your whole city, province or state. Continue radiating loving kindness to your whole country, your continent and finally to the whole world and all its beings.

In a traditional Buddhist sense, send loving kindness first to your parents, grandparents, elders and teachers. Then send loving kindness to your siblings, spouse, children and other family members. Continue radiating loving kindness to friends, colleagues, associates and so on, including people you don't know and with whom you have no relationship. As your compassion deepens, send it equally to your enemies and anyone you have harmed or has caused you harm. Radiate healing compassion to all beings with equal sincerity. This practice opens your heart wider and wider to heal all of life in every manifestation. Remember to send loving kindness to your own being.

Sending loving kindness during meditation does not excuse us from making amends on a personal basis through apologies and forgiveness. Radiating loving kindness and compassion to all beings is a positive step towards meeting your adversaries face to face with a kind smile.

**Planetary Health Care**

What if our planet had cancer? Diabetes? Heart disease? High blood pressure? AIDS? Depression? This topic can inspire an empowering workshop if you have an opportunity to share this topic with friends, colleagues or students in your community.

To begin, the whole group brainstorms questions such as: What is the nature of this disease? What is its symbolic meaning? How can we treat it? How can it be prevented? Organise into groups of three to six people for discussion. Each group selects one disease for analysis and answers the questions as effectively as possible. Afterwards, the whole group joins together to share their findings. Finally, reflect on how the topic of planetary health informs us concerning our personal health.

In response to the above questions during a recent course on sustainable development in Thailand, participants elicited several profound practices designed to heal our planet. What if our planet had cancer? Suggestions included employing indigenous wisdom, rejuvenating nature, establishing a new value system in family and community, practicing perma-culture and sustainable use of resources, learning from elders, celebrating the positive, controlling greed, and awareness raising on all these issues. It was a truly inspiring learning session among participants from China, Indonesia, Britain and a dozen other countries. We concluded that in addition to practicing mindfulness, we also needed to understand the concept of "planetfulness."

We are the mind,
The consciousness of this planet,
Incarnate.

## Planetary Responsibilities

Is there any limit to healing? This book advances a concept of healing that embraces the entire scope of personal transformation. These pages have been dedicated to healing self and others. The culmination of this process aims towards planetary healing. This suggests using every aspect of existence as a tool towards nurturing the planet. The question of healing is no longer limited to healing the individual self, but expands towards healing life as a whole.

Consider the following questions and how to foster transformation on a personal or planetary level. Choose a particular situation in which you are involved and make it the subject of today's reflection. You may raise these questions in your written meditation, or suggest them at community gatherings or seminars.

1. To what degree does this behaviour benefit humanity?
2. Does this activity nurture or damage the environment?
3. Do I actively create the world in which I claim to be a mere victim?

Discuss these topics with your community and see what insights are raised. Another process that you can lead with your Reiki community is to collectively send energy to trouble spots in the world such as earthquake zones or regions suffering civil unrest. Sit in a circle together and join hands. If it helps, place a photo or news article in the middle of your circle as a reference point to focus your group's attention. All members visualise the recipients or the troubled area and send distance healing simultaneously. Visualise all three of the Reiki symbols and send them just as you would send distance healing to a person.

Another way to extend the realm of Reiki healing is to bring your healing community outdoors to perform planetary healings. Group members place their hands on trees, stones or water to represent the whole earth. If weather doesn't permit you to sit outside, perform the same ritual using a houseplant as representative of the earth. Visualise Reiki healing the earth in every direction. You are the universe, so, the practice of healing the universe is the logical extension of self healing.

## Universal Meditation

I'd like to review the process of meditation as we approach the conclusion of this book. Meditation awakens and transforms your consciousness, moving you from self-centred ego towards universal self. The illusion of an individual self is gainfully employed due to the continuity of thought. The more we generate thoughts, the busier we become mentally. Then we become even more convinced of our individual existence. The more we are obsessed by individual self, the less awareness we generate towards universal self.

In Andean cosmology, by becoming invisible, the Shaman truly masters healing. Healing is a transpersonal process that transcends the personal ego of the healer. In the Buddhist sense, this is referred to as Anatta, the impersonal non-self. By releasing attachment to ego, we become one with the universe and energy flows unimpeded. Meditation calms the mind and prevents the mind from jumping around. This is especially important when doing distance Reiki healings where strong focus is required.

Meditation increases energy and vitality, giving the skill to overcome depression, anger, fear and other mental barriers that prevent us from perceiving the divine order. Meditation helps us become aware of negative thought patterns and habits, and thus overcome them. It also helps us overcome attachment to positive thoughts and feelings that trap us in the realm of pleasure. Taken together, being mindful of positive, neutral and negative tendencies, meditation moves us from a doing mode into a being mode. This generates greater peace and equanimity in our minds and fosters contentment with what we have, rather than obsessing over what we want. This is the path to realising our true essence.

A very powerful meditation practice is known as "Atitan." Atitan refers to making a vow to yourself to sit in meditation for one hour without moving so much as a finger. Holding still and stable in the lotus position for a solid hour is an intense challenge. It can be painful, boring or blissful. Whatever arises, be with it. No need to struggle against it; just be there with the feelings. One hour in perfectly still silent meditation can seem like an eternity. Take it one breath at a time, always knowing the breath inhaling and exhaling. Pain and boredom are your guides during Atitan meditation because each time you notice these feelings you are reminded to return your focus to the present breath.

One of the best books I've studied concerning meditation is "Mindfulness in Plain English" by Venerable H. Gunaratana Mahathera. He advises mediators to explore the process of breathing as a vehicle for realising our inherent connectedness with the rest of life by emphasising the universal factors of life. He explains that "mindfulness practice is the practice of 100 percent honesty with ourselves. If we mindfully investigate our own minds, we discover bitter truths in ourselves. That is, we are selfish, egocentric, attached to our egos, holding on to opinions, we think we're right and everybody else is wrong, we're biased and do not really love ourselves." God, it sounds like he's talking about me!

What about you? At first, these insights might seem very bitter and pessimistic, but long term, this discovery delivers us from deeply rooted psychological and spiritual suffering. We slowly become aware of what we truly are deep down inside by listening to our own thoughts, but not getting caught up in them. I find that deep meditation during a period of fasting is a powerful combination that brings deeply rooted emotional issues to the surface. Once they arise into consciousness they can be perceived clearly for what they are. Such feelings can also be released without further adieu.

Purification of the body through fasting, of the mind through meditation, and our whole being through Reiki, inspire the Grace of awakening into our original essence.

Meditation is participatory observation. You actually become the breath, rather than being a passive observer. To come full circle, let's return to our discussion of quantum physics from the first chapter. What you observe responds to your act of observation. Quantum physicists struggle with the same paradox when observing quantum activity: An object or event has multiple potentials; its actual state is determined by interaction with the observer. In meditation, you are both the observer and the observed; there is no distinction. Vipassana meditation is not about pondering. It's about being. Don't ponder. Just be. Once you start pondering, you get all caught up in thoughts. The truth is you don't need to figure everything out. Discursive thinking won't free you from the trap. The mind is purified naturally by mindfulness, by wordless, bare attention.

Although meditation becomes much more complex as you gain experience, I will boil it down to a few clear steps to support you in your practice. If you have read this whole book but not practised any of the meditation techniques, well… I can't meditate for you! I can only suggest that you review these steps, close your eyes and take the next breath in your personal evolution:

- Meditate twice a day as regularly as possible
- Meditation at dawn and dusk are optimum times
- Sit cross-legged or in lotus position if possible
- Keep as still as you can
- Keep your back straight
- Observe the breath as it passes through the nostrils or expands the diaphragm
- When the mind wanders, bring it back to observing the breath

- Allow each thought to arise and pass without attachment
- Observe all sensations with equanimity
- Observe feelings from the perspective of the universe, rather than from a personal perspective
- Conclude by sharing compassion with all beings

Over time, you will probably want to consult with an experienced monk or meditation master to guide you in your practice. When you are ready, consider a deeper commitment to meditation by attending a 7 to 10 day retreat with a meditation master to practise intensely.

## Blessings

Thank you for taking the time and effort to pursue your personal transformation through Reiki. It's a long path, as elegant as it is demanding. I trust this text has been helpful in pointing out some of the salient features of the terrain as you discover the nature and texture of your deepest self. Thank you for your contribution to healing yourself, healing others, healing humanity and our planet.

If you get a chance, you might like to visit our Organic Reiki Ashram in Chiang Mai, Thailand where we practise all the topics in this book as well as grow our own organic fruits and vegetables. This will be the subject of a future chapter on personal transformation…

References and a bibliography are included below to provide you with many of the road maps to healing and health that have been laid before you. The next step, like every step, depends on you. Be healthy.

# Afterword

It might seem that Reiki, Yoga, Taiji, Pranayama and religion are all distinct and separate from each other. The only thing that actually separates them are the time, place and culture in which they were originally conceived or systematised. Isn't it quite likely that Buddha practised Yoga? Is it reasonable to suggest that Jesus healed his followers using the same loving energy described by Reiki and Taiji? Are the hygienic precepts in the Christian, Hindu, Islamic and Jewish traditions consistent with the principles of Naturopathy and Veganism?

    While humans seem inclined to systematise and categorise, this causes division and separation. Why can't we bring ancient and modern traditions of health and wisdom from East and West into our present lives whether we live North or South. Can you adopt these practices even while embracing and being true to your personal faith? Why do we construct barriers that limit or even betray us?

While you may be ready to close this book, life itself remains an open book. I hope this one has succeeded in building bridges between these disciplines and made them accessible from your front door. At the same time, please forgive me if I have trampled too roughly on the lawn or stepped on some toes in the process of this construction. I hope this text serves to present an authentic holistic approach even while some points have aimed to discredit certain modern ideologies. I trust this book truly aspires to the universal, while knowing it is rooted in my own ego. When I get a little wiser, I'll return to patch all the differences. Peace.

# Annotated Bibliography

"Animal Reiki" by Elizabeth Fulton and Kathleen Prasad (Ulysses Press, 2006) explains techniques for using Reiki with all types of animals from dogs to deer.

"The Art and Science of Raja Yoga" by Swami Kriyananda (Hansa Trust, 2002) thoroughly explains all aspects of Yoga including postures, breathing, healing, nutrition and meditation.

"Awaken Healing Energy through the Tao" by Mantak Chia (Aurora Press, 1991) explains how to awaken and circulate life force energy through the meridians of the body for physical, psychological and spiritual health.

"Being Peace" by Thich Nhat Hanh (Parallax Press, 2005) presents Buddhism and mindfulness in its true simplicity while reaching into deeper truths. This is an excellent book for beginning mindfulness and meditation.

"The Conquest of Cancer" by Dr. Virginia Livingston-Wheeler (Franklin Watts, 1983) explains how a strong diet contributes to strong immunity.

"Conscious Eating" by Gabriel Cousens, M.D. (North Atlantic Books, 2000) is the most informative and inspiring book I have found that explains every dimension of meat based and vegetable based diets, including analysis of spiritual and environmental issues.

"The Crystal Bible" by Judy Hall (Godsfield Press, 2003) is a comprehensive source concerning the qualities and healing applications of a wide variety of crystals.

"Cutting through Spiritual Materialism" by Chogyam Trungpa (Shambhala Publications, 1973) challenges beliefs considered "holy" by showing how materialistic values intrude into spiritual practice.

"Death by Prescription" by Ray D. Strand, M.D. (Magna Publishing, 2004) investigates how the use of prescription drugs has become the third leading cause of death in the United States. This is essential reading before you accept your doctor's next prescription.

"Diet for a New America" by John Robbins (HJ Kramer, 1998) exposes industrial farming practices and how these contribute to serious health issues.

Drugs.Com (2018) provides information on the side effects of pharmaceutical drugs at http://www.drugs.com/sfx/

"Eastern Body, Western Mind" by Anodea Judith (Celestial Arts, 2004) is the primary source for much of the chakra information in chapter four. This is an authoritative source that explains each chakra in detail plus extensive techniques for developing and healing each one.

"Entangled Minds: Extrasensory Experiences in a Quantum Reality" by Dean Radin (Paraview Pocket Books, 2006) explains the physical reality behind telepathy and intuition. He provides a scientific explanation for psychic phenomena.

"Essential Reiki" by Diane Stein (The Crossing Press, Inc. 1995) thoroughly explains Reiki 1, 2 and 3 with an extensive description of the ancient history of Reiki and its relationship to Buddhism.

"The Eye of the I" by David Hawkins (Veritas Publishing, 2001) effectively employs science to understand spirituality and expansion of consciousness.

Food Democracy (http://fooddemocracy.wordpress.com) (2018) is based on the slogan "The right of all people to an adequate, safe, nutritious, sustainable, food supply."

"The Guide for the Perplexed" by E.F. Schumacher (Harper Perennial, 1978) challenges traditional science in an effort to stimulate the full realisation of human potential.

"Healing Touch, A Guidebook for Practitioners" by Dorothea Hover-Kramer (Delmar Publishers, 2002) is the source for some of the additional healing techniques in chapter three.

"Listen to your Body" by Bisong Guo and Andrew Powell (University of Hawai'i Press, 2001) offers a clear and simple explanation of very profound Daoist philosophy and methods for improving the quality of your life.

"Livestock's Long Shadow" (Food and Agricultural Organisation of the United Nations, 2006) explains the environmental impacts of raising cattle and livestock.

"Living with Diabetes the Reiki Way" by Kathie Lipinski, RN (Reiki News Magazine, Spring 2007) explains research involving the application of Reiki with diabetes patients.

"The Lost Steps of Reiki, the Channelled Teachings of Wei Chi" by Thomas Hensel and Kevin Ross Emery (Light Lines Publishing, 1997) describes the inter-active nature of Reiki.

"The Message from Water" by Masaru Emoto (HADO Kyoikusha, Tokyo, 1999) demonstrates the influence of consciousness and language on the structure of water crystals. His photos are works of art that visually demonstrate the power of thought.

"Mindfulness-Based Cognitive Therapy for Depression" by Zindel V. Segal, J. Mark G. Williams, and John D. Teasdale (Guildford Press, 2002) explains the effectiveness of practicing mindfulness for treating depression.

"Mindfulness in Plain English" by Venerable Henepola Gunaratana Mahathera (Wave Imprint, 1991) clearly explains the subtle meaning and practice of mindfulness.

"The Miracle of Mindfulness" by Thich Nhat Hanh (Parallax Press, 1999) provides a beautiful discussion of mindfulness meditation techniques and practices.

Nisargopchar Ashram (http://www.nisargopcharashram.org/) (2018) was founded by Mahatma Gandhi in Pune, India. This is where we studied Naturopathy in 2010 with Dr. Ravindra Nisal.

Nature Life Hospital (http://naturelifeinternational.com/) (2018) in Kerala, India is under the direction of Dr. Jacob Vadakkanchery. Visit the website for compelling insights into the healing power of nature and fasting for health.

Natural News (www.Naturalnews.com) (2018) presents articles focusing on natural living and exposes the dangers of Genetically Modified Organisms (GMOs) in our food supply.

Organic Consumers Organization (http://www.organicconsumers.org) (2018) campaigns for health, justice, sustainability, peace and democracy.

"Owner's Manual for the Human Body" by Yogi Bhajan (Kundalini Research Institute, 1998) provides a variety of Kundalini exercises for personal development.

People for the Ethical Treatment of Animals (http://www.peta.org) (2018) provides information concerning Vegan ethics, lifestyle and several videos documenting the suffering of animals.

"Plants as Teachers" by Matthew Wood (North Atlantic Books, 1987) discusses how nature teaches and heals us.

"Psychic Discoveries behind the Iron Curtain" (Bantam Books, 1970) explores decades of research in the Soviet Union concerning psychic testing, dowsing, energy healing and Kirlian photography.

Reiki Advice from Thailand (http://reikiadvicefromthailand.blogspot.com/) (2018) answers students' questions concerning Reiki.

Reiki Chiang Mai (https://sites.google.com/site/reikichiangmai/) (2018) is an organic Reiki ashram in northern Thailand where the author teaches and heals with holistic Reiki practice.

"The Secret Life of Plants" by Peter Tompkins and Christopher Bird (Rupa Publications, 2004) presents a fascinating history of research concerning the consciousness of plants and the relationship between human consciousness and nature.

"Self-Discovery and Self-Healing" by Dr. John Upledger in "Healers on Healing" (Jeremy P. Tarcher, 1989) describes his insightful concept of healing.

"Selling Sickness: How the World's Biggest Pharmaceutical Companies are Turning us all into Patients" by Ray Moynihan and Alan Cassels (Nation Books, 2005) examines how modern day "diseases" are designed, defined or invented to increase drug sales.

"Spontaneous Healing" by Andrew Weil (Ballantine Publishing, 1995) discusses a variety of non-toxic ways to optimise your health.

"The Tao of Physics" by Fritjof Capra (Shambhala Publications, 1975) explores parallels between modern physics and Eastern mysticism.

"World as Lover, World as Self" by Joanna Macy (Parallax Press, 2005) describes how seeing the world as oneself, or as a lover, transforms ordinary reality and provides a greater sense of purpose.

"The 8 Limbs of Yoga" by Bhava Ram (Deep Yoga, 2010) explores Yoga far beyond the postures; he focuses on morality, non-violence, control of life forces and mindfulness based on Patanjali's Yoga Sutras.

# About the Author

Reiki Master Tom Radzienda has healed patients and taught Reiki to students from all over the world including Argentina, Bolivia, England, Holland, India, Russia, Thailand, the United States and Venezuela. In 2006, he served as a volunteer healer at "Mosoq Runa" children's home in Urubamba, Perú. In 2007 and 2008, he was a volunteer Reiki teacher and healer at "Moo Bahn Dek" Children's Village in Kanjanaburi, Thailand. Since 2008 he has been teaching Reiki, providing healing and counselling in Bangkok. He now facilitates holistic Reiki health courses at his Reiki Centre in Chiang Mai, Thailand.

Tom has studied Vipassana meditation in Thailand and Perú, practicing daily for many years. He also has experience in Taiji, Yoga, Veganism, Naturopathy, Tarot, use of crystals and pendulums. He combines these techniques with Reiki to the optimum benefit of each student and patient.

Tom is also an accomplished writer, poet and lecturer. He holds the post of Assistant Professor at Srinakharinwirot University in Bangkok where he taught Western culture, poetry and media analysis from 1994 to 2006. He has published five books including "Essence," "Luxuries of Grace," "Fire Dreams," "A Promise for Siam" and "No More Pretty Pictures." He has also served as columnist for the Bangkok Post. His column Poet's Post featured poetry and photography while Poet's Post was designed for the benefit of students and teachers of poetry.

He can be reached by email at tomradzienda@gmail.com

www.ingramcontent.com/pod-product-compliance
Lightning Source LLC
Chambersburg PA
CBHW060319050426
42449CB00011B/2549